Gerald W. McEntee

The Heart of a Lion

By Francis Ryan

Washington, D.C., 2012

Copyright © 2012 by AFSCME

All rights reserved. No part of this publication may be reproduced in any form or by any means, electronic or mechanical, without written permission from the publisher except in the case of brief quotations embodied in critical articles and reviews.

Library of Congress Control Number: 2012938920
ISBN: 978-0-9855633-0-1

Published by American Federation of State, County and
Municipal Employees (AFSCME), AFL-CIO
1625 L Street, NW, Washington, D.C. 20036
(202) 429-1051

Printed in the United States by union labor.

First Edition: June 2012

Dedication

Over the past 15 years of working on the history of AFSCME, I've had the opportunity to collaborate with hundreds of union members at regional leadership training conferences, Next Wave and International Conventions, and retiree gatherings. I dedicate this book to all the many friends I've made among AFSCME's members from around the country. Meeting and working with you will always be the best part of what I do as a labor historian.

— Francis Ryan

Contents

Foreward 7
Chapter 1 — The Boy From Swampoodle 11
Chapter 2 — The AFSCME Connection 17
Chapter 3 — The Push for Collective Bargaining 23
Chapter 4 — In the Political Mix 29
Chapter 5 — The Young Organizer 35
Chapter 6 — Memphis 1968 47
Chapter 7 — Driving AFSCME to the Forefront 51
Chapter 8 — Tackling Pennsylvania 59
Chapter 9 — Building on Success. 71
Chapter 10 — Taking a Big Step Up 85
Chapter 11 — Expanding AFSCME 93
Chapter 12 — Target: National Political Influence 97
Chapter 13 — The Revolt in the AFL-CIO 105
Chapter 14 — Expanding the Union's Horizon 113
Chapter 15 — Combating Corruption 121
Chapter 16 — The New Millennium 125
Chapter 17 — Struggling Through Destruction and Death 133
Chapter 18 — Challenging Bush 137
Chapter 19 — Blending Old and New Methods for a New Age 145
Chapter 20 — The 2008 Election 151
Chapter 21 — Years of Challenge and Hope 155
Chapter 22 — Building a Main Street Movement 159
Chapter 23 — The End of an Era 165
Acknowledgments 173

Photographs follow page 96.

Foreword

By Lee A. Saunders

Shortly before the 2006 election, President Bill Clinton was speaking at a rally in Milwaukee, Wisconsin, when he saw Jerry McEntee with a group of AFSCME members in the crowd. Clinton, a dues-paying member of AFSCME while he was governor of Arkansas, took a moment to talk about the union's early endorsement of his candidacy in 1992. It was an endorsement that helped propel the young governor into the lead among the Democratic contenders and eventually into the White House.

Clinton said that the crowd wouldn't know it, but "Jerry McEntee took a huge chance" when our union endorsed him. At that moment in the '92 campaign, Clinton was running fifth in the field of six candidates in the New Hampshire primary.

"Only my mother thought I could win. Hillary and Chelsea were still down as undecided," he mentioned to laughter from the crowd.

Jerry McEntee had made the difference. "He has the heart of a lion," President Clinton summed up, "and I never had a better friend."

When it was suggested that the "heart of a lion" phrase be part of the title of this short biography, Jerry tried to veto the idea. He thought it was too grandiose. Jerry McEntee isn't grand. He is plain spoken. But he has always been a fighter. That's why President Clinton's phrase "the heart of a lion" rings true. It reflects the fighting spirit that Jerry has shown throughout his remarkable career.

AFSCME members have seen his big heart and fighting spirit in every corner of this country. They know that he has fought for them, for their families, for their communities, and for this country we all love. He has fought to give working men and women a voice on the job, good pay and benefits and a secure retirement.

In this book, Professor Francis Ryan captures some key moments in those fights. The book is by no means comprehensive. No short treatment could include every organizing battle, every legislative effort or every political campaign. Nor does the book focus on Jerry's personal life and the loving support he has received from Barbara and his four wonderful daughters — Patty, Kelly, Kathy and Chris. They know the sacrifices Jerry has made during his long career with AFSCME.

BY LEE A. SAUNDERS

What this book does is provide a brief portrait of a man and his mission. It serves as a reminder of why Jerry McEntee's leadership has made such a difference, to our union and to our country. No labor leader has been more committed, more strategic and more relentless when it comes to standing up for the rights of America's workers.

The passion, drive and spirit he brought to every contest is on full display here — from his boyhood in Swampoodle through his first organizing campaigns. From the fight for health care reform to the struggle to preserve collective bargaining against relentless right-wing attacks. From pension protection and women's rights to workplace safety and anti-privatization fights, Jerry McEntee always stood up, and he always spoke out.

Every step of the way, Jerry has fought for the rights of our members — and to find ways to move AFSCME and the entire labor movement forward.

Solidarity is more than a word to Jerry. It has been his life's mission. I have known him for more than three decades. He's been a mentor and a true friend. I know what a difference he has made for our members and all working families in this country. You will see that in the pages of this remarkable book.

He's been a leader with unmatched skill, undiminished vision and untiring strength. Now, as he begins a well-deserved retirement, his big heart and fighting spirit will continue to inspire AFSCME members across America. Jerry McEntee has fought hard for us.

He proved year in and year out that he was a leader with enormous talent, unrivaled instincts and an unconquerable passion for the cause of working men and women.

Through all these years, Jerry has been a true believer. He believed in the men and women of AFSCME, and he believed in the working men and women of America.

He believed in our ability to organize and to fight for our rights. He believed in the American Dream. And he fought like hell to make sure it survives for generations to come.

Bill Clinton was right.

Jerry McEntee has the heart of a lion.

1

The Boy From Swampoodle

Everyone knew that Philadelphia's sanitation routes involved men's work. Those who did it spent more than ten hours a day on three-man trucks or horse-drawn wagons, lifting tons of rubbish and coal ash left on the curbs by householders who took them pretty much for granted. Beyond the public view, others shared in this labor. In the dim cellars of the city's working-class homes, the wives, mothers and daughters of Philadelphia's sanitation workers played important supporting roles.

For example, in a small, three-story brick home on Bambrey Street, in the city's Swampoodle section, Mary McEntee squeezed out the work clothes of her husband Bill who drove one of these trucks for the city. In these pails, her hands wrinkled and hardened with the soot and ash that turned water a soapy brown. She was part of her husband's work.

By the mid-1930s, this section of North Philadelphia had expanded to become one of the city's most densely populated and industrialized areas. Entirely working class, it consisted of homes of working men and women arrayed along narrow, treeless streets within walking distance of the mills and warehouses and train yards where they were employed. The McEntee family had settled here just at the beginning of the Great Depression, fortunate to survive the economic downfall with the low-paying but steady truck driver job Bill had maintained with Philadelphia's Street Cleaning Bureau.

In 1935, the young couple celebrated the birth of a son, Gerald William McEntee, who they would always call Jerry. Just a generation before he was born, this section of North Philadelphia was mostly vacant lots and open fields, with inhabitants described by Philadelphia historian Bruce Kucklick as "often Irish, many recent immigrants or refugees from Pennsylvania coalfields." The area near Swampoodle was known to Philadelphians mostly for its proximity to Shibe Park, the home of the Athletics baseball team. Along with the ballpark, Swampoodle was, by World War I, one of the most industrialized sections of the city; the Pennsylvania Railroad crisscrossed a network of smaller but busy lines that carried passengers as well as the industrial wares that came from the region's hundreds of textile mills, factories, dye houses and warehouses.

Here, in this industrial world of Swampoodle, the McEntees were no different than any other working class family. People on Bambrey Street all worked in local industries. One neighbor was a steel hand at Midvale Steel Works in the city's

East Falls section; a woman across the street, a waitress at a nearby diner; the man next door, a bus driver for the Philadelphia Transit Company. Many worked more than one job — sometimes three — to make ends meet. After his ten-hour hour shifts on the trash routes, Bill McEntee did a part-time job hauling barrows of coal at a nearby firm.

This neighborhood was racially and ethnically diverse, but certain traits were common. Like working people across the nation, this generation — on the eve of the Great Depression — lacked economic security. As historian David Kennedy notes, "They worked feverishly when times were good, when the mills were roaring and the forges hot, in order to lay something away against the inevitable moment when times would turn bad, when the factory gates would swing shut and the furnaces be banked. The unpredictable perturbations in their lives constantly disrupted relations among family members and left little opportunity for social or civic involvement, or even for trade union organization. This precarious, disconnected, socially thin, pervasively insecure way of life was the lot of millions of Americans in the 1920s."

With the collapse of the national economy in 1929, the stability of American workers disappeared. By 1933, Philadelphia's political world had been transformed, as thousands of voters left the Republican Party, which had ruled almost since the end of the Civil War, in favor of the New Deal promises of newly elected President Franklin Delano Roosevelt. In response to his call for the nation's workers to join labor unions, thousands of Philadelphians did so — forming powerful organizations that represented the full diversity of the fabled Workshop of the World — from subway drivers and taxi cab operators to beauticians, steelworker, candy makers and supermarket clerks.

The men who collected Philadelphia's trash and swept its streets were perhaps the least likely group to join the ranks of organized labor. Even with the advances made under President Roosevelt, the city's local government and its vast patronage system were controlled by the most powerful Republican political machine in the United States. City workers answered to political bosses and their stooges, who demanded unpaid service in mobilizing the vote in the neighborhoods where they lived, and mandatory contributions of a portion of their annual salaries to the local Republican club.

Considered by many citizens to be social pariahs for their work with trash — with its associated smells and diseases — the trash haulers and sweepers were not even reckoned by some to be in the ranks of organized labor. But when political bosses fired over 200 sanitation and street repair laborers in September 1938, almost 3,000 city workers waged an eight-day strike that brought the city's essential services to a halt. In one of the most violent strikes of that era, sanitation workers and their families fought against scabs and police officers, waging daylong battles on the streets of North Philadelphia.

Among the most militant leaders of the strike was Jerry's father, William J. McEntee. In the 1938 actions, by organizing squadrons of strikers to fight against scabs on the sanitation routes, he established his leadership credentials. Under Bill McEntee's direction, the striking workers affiliated with the American Federation of Labor (AFL) just before a settlement was reached, joining an organization neither he nor most of his fellow strikers had ever heard of — the newly chartered American Federation of State, County and Municipal Employees (AFSCME).

2

The AFSCME Connection

Tracing its roots back to 1932, when a group of Wisconsin state employees (later to become AFSCME Council 24) formed an organization to fight an incoming political administration's effort to terminate their jobs, AFSCME stood out as one of the most unusual unions of the New Deal era. Excluded from the protection of new federal labor law, which viewed government employees as different from workers in the private sector, the union positioned itself as an organization that sought implementation of civil service reforms. In October 1936, the AFL chartered the national American Federation of State, County and Municipal Employees.

AFSCME's founder, Arnold S. Zander, stood apart from most of the new industrial trade union leaders of his generation, having attained a doctorate from the University of Wisconsin and specializing in organizing white collar, professional workers. Under his direction, AFSCME built an information-clearing house at its national headquarters in Madison in order to educate workers, politicians and taxpayers on the need for professional administrative services in government, and set about building a national organization.

Philadelphia proved one of the most unusual battlegrounds for the new government workers union. Following the 1938 strike, Bill McEntee helped shape AFSCME into a fast-growing and militant union. Through the early 1930s, the union threatened numerous strikes, and held a two-week walkout in early 1944 to secure a wage increase of a dime an hour.

That year, Bill McEntee was elected the first president of AFSCME District Council 33, the newly formed umbrella group that housed the numerous locals that made up the union in the city. McEntee placed great emphasis on political engagement, and in 1947, he helped launch a political reform movement that succeeded in overthrowing the corrupt Republican machine that had ruled Philadelphia for more than a generation.

Through these years of AFSCME's development in Philadelphia, watching his father develop the new labor organization into a political force, Jerry McEntee learned the nature of political power and its use. At home, he also learned lessons about the importance of solidarity and justice.

Among the values he picked up in this world were the value of hard work, and the importance of family. The boy grew up with his sister Mary among his neighborhood's working class children, attending St. Columba's grade school and later Roman Catholic High School. Decades later, he could still arouse laughter from AFSCME staffers with stories from his youth, including his ongoing love of Tastykakes and his uncle's unsafe driving habits: "He was a rich Republican who continued to drive even when he lost much of his eyesight. He'd rely on his memory of the roads."

In his days before starting college, McEntee earned money in the summers at Wildwood, New Jersey. Working for a beach umbrella and chair vendor, his got his first taste of organizing. "I worked in Wildwood, on the beach, renting umbrellas and chairs. That was great, you got a tan, all the other kids would be there on the beach. It was a wonderful experience."

But there was an issue, and McEntee tackled it. "We were supposed to have rainy days off," he recalls. "You had no days off unless it rained. That was a clear part of the agreement. We had twenty-five days of sunshine, and then it rained. That morning, I'm lying in bed, thinking I didn't have to go to work when a couple of guys I worked with showed up and woke me up. They said we had to go stitch umbrellas. I went in. But I took everyone out on strike. I got fired, and they all stayed."

In 1952, McEntee enrolled at La Salle College. Located just a few subway stops from his home, La Salle had, from 1938-44, been the center of one of Philadelphia's important workers education programs: the La Salle College Civic and Social Congress, organized by Brother Elzear Alfred Kelly, a member of the Christian Brothers order. The congress specialized in introducing the new set of labor leaders to practical training in economics, American politics, public speaking and labor law.

One of those new leaders was Bill McEntee, who attended Brother Alfred's classes throughout the program's existence. With that strong connection to the college, Jerry McEntee thrived at La Salle, majoring in economics with the legendary Professor Joseph Flubacher. These courses connected his studies with his developing love of the political world. The college was also an exciting place in the mid-1950s: the Explorers basketball team was a national powerhouse, winning both the National Invitational Tournament and the NCAA.

After graduating from La Salle in 1956 and a doing a six-month stint in the U.S. Army, McEntee went to work with the City of Philadelphia's Bureau of Traffic Engineering. They gave him a car and assigned him to monitor various intersections, "checking the volume of cars going through to determine if a particular one should have a stop sign or traffic light." This position marked the beginning of the young man's formal membership in AFSCME.

As a new employee, McEntee joined Local 427 (District Council 33), and quickly became involved in union activities. He had many conversations about how to strengthen the union's power within the Quaker City and how to expand into a range of other, unorganized departments within the municipal government.

By the late 1950s, DC 33 was widely recognized as a national trailblazer among AFSCME's councils. Having secured strong contracts with pension benefits and job security through their proven militancy in the 1930s and '40s, Philadelphia's Municipal Workers Union was now breaking new ground in securing health and welfare benefits: hospitalization for members and their entire families, including a dental and eye care provision, services unprecedented in units elsewhere in the United States.

Working with other visionary labor leaders in the region, Bill McEntee and other council leaders proposed an even bolder health care program — a union-owned and administered hospital. Building the financial assets for this venture with federal grants and deposits by union members across the city, AFSCME finally realized this plan in 1962, with the construction of a union hospital (soon renamed in honor of President John F. Kennedy, the slain leader who had championed collective bargaining rights for public employees).

These advancements in Philadelphia were matched by fresh efforts on the parts of AFSCME leaders across the United States. Wisconsin — the historic home of the union — achieved new legal status when the union achieved formal collective bargaining rights in 1959, setting the stage for similar campaigns in other states. While still relatively small and regional compared to industrial unions like the Steelworkers and Autoworkers, some industrial relations experts observed that AFSCME would become the union of the future.

Jerry McEntee's conversations with his father about the future of the union inspired him to become more involved with it. Although Bill McEntee did not encourage his son to pursue a career in the labor movement, he was proud of that decision.

Late in 1956, the young McEntee came on staff as an organizer and economic advisor. "I went down to Washington D.C. to meet with the director of organizing, and he hired me for a peanut. I don't know if AFSCME had much of an organizing strategy at that time."

3

The Push for Collective Bargaining

Jerry McEntee's first assignment was with District Council 33, working as a political and economic advisor, and developing organizing strategies. One of his more important tasks was working with the city's growing finance and clerical section, Local 696. Originally organized in 1951 by Charlie Santore, a Republican ward leader from South Philadelphia, Local 696 had a base of close to 600 members, mostly clerical employees in Philadelphia's city hall as well as its revenue departments and libraries. Having studied modern industrial relations at La Salle, McEntee found the operations with Santore's local to be much more informal — and behind the times — than those of the standard union.

"Local 696 — compared to what unions are today — was entirely different." McEntee recalls. "At DC 33, and really, in most government workplaces across the country, there was no such thing as union shops, no such thing as even standard grievance procedures: everything was informal. The founder of Local 696, Charlie Santore was business agent and Buhrman Smith was president. They were great people, but they didn't really know how to run a union. I helped them run that phase of the union."

One point everyone in the union agreed on was the need to expand the local's membership. With the majority of Philadelphia's clerical workers still unorganized, McEntee developed strategies to expand Local 696 into what could become one of the council's largest sections. The local was growing, and McEntee propelled the process. But because the task of meeting with workers at their offices or in the workplaces was daunting, he developed proposals to bring workers in through a legislative process. In April 1958, DC 33 inaugurated the largest organizing campaign in its history, seeking to net 7,000 city employees. According to Local 403 business agent John Miller, the council aimed "to sign up every city employee in each of the city's 28 departments in District Council 33."

Political alliances would prove vital in this campaign. AFSCME, with just under 10,000 members ranked as one of the largest and most powerful unions in the city. In addition, it had developed close ties with the city's powerful Building Trades Council and Teamsters locals, and could count on their vocal support. Most important, AFSCME had built strong ties with the Democratic Party. The union had worked closely with Mayor Richardson Dilworth in encouraging members to participate in door-to-door voter registration campaigns and get-out-the-vote operations. After several years of lobbying the mayor, and with support from the city's Central Labor Union, legislation passed. In April 1961, Mayor Dilworth supported an ordinance that granted DC 33 a modified union shop, establishing three categories: mandatory (blue collar) voluntary (supervisors, technical and professional) and prohibited (administrators and uniformed).

AFSCME's successes in Philadelphia were replicated elsewhere. In cities and states around the country, increasing numbers of government workers were looking to public sector unions as ways to secure basic rights. Since the shift in national labor legislation during the New Deal, public workers had remained outside the protection of laws that protected organizing and strike actions, but this was changing. In the new generation's emphasis on rights, public workers stepped forward. Public attitudes toward workers' organizations had been changing during the post-war period, including a growing acceptance of government unionization.

In Washington, a significant development was President John F. Kennedy's Task Force on Employee-Management Relations in the Federal Service, which led to the new policy in favor of federal government union organizing. In 1962, Kennedy signed Executive Order 10988. On the fiftieth anniversary of the signing of the order, Georgetown University Professor Joseph McCartin noted in the *Los Angeles Times* that the effects of Kennedy's order were much more extensive than just on federal employees.

"At the time Kennedy acted, very few workers at any level of government had won the right to bargain collectively with their employers," McCartin wrote. "Federal action helped inspire many states and localities to follow suit, allowing their own workers to organize. This triggered a huge wave of unionization in the public sector that saw firefighters, teachers, sanitation workers, social workers and many others form unions in the 1960s and '70s."

Teachers' unions, long minor players in American labor, emerged suddenly as a powerful force in reshaping legal attitudes toward the unionized civil servant. Following a contract impasse in 1967, New York's United Federation of Teachers president, Albert Shanker, took teachers out on strike. The militancy initiated a change in tactics for teachers around the country. In Philadelphia, public school teachers gained collective bargaining rights for the first time, and affiliated with the American Federation of Teachers as Local 3, negotiating their first contract the same year. By the end of the decade, the AFT and the National Education Association were two of the largest unions in the country.

Of all the national unions of government employees, AFSCME's potential seemed the greatest. Arnold Zander, at the 1960 AFSCME Convention, announced an ambitious organizing initiative that would bring in half a million members by the end of the decade. While all agreed on the desirability of such a goal, there was deep disagreement over how to achieve it. At this point, many found Zander, who had run the union since its founding, disconnected from average members and focused on international programs of the Public Service International that often took him out of the country. For example, Zander did not go to Alabama to support a series of public employee strikes.

Increasing numbers of AFSCME members pushed for change. Leading AFSCME's growing dissident faction was the brash and militant leader of New York City's District Council 37, Jerry Wurf. Since coming into the union in 1944, he had taken a small and badly divided 37 and made it the nation's largest urban chapter.

Wurf had broken with Zander over the direction AFSCME should take in the 1960s and beyond. Instead of focusing on civil service provisions, Wurf believed, AFSCME should become a fighting organization to empower its members through the kinds of political pressure and militant tactics long used by the nation's more powerful industrial unions. Ultimately, the growing political power of unionized, government employees would focus on attempting to shape a broader social transformation that would bring the basic necessities of life to all Americans. Following two unsuccessful bids at replacing Zander, Wurf narrowly won the International presidency in 1964.

The period after Wurf's victory 1964 saw a remarkable shift in the union's power. Arriving at the AFSCME headquarters in Washington D.C., Wurf instituted a series of changes. At a symbolic level, Wurf he changed AFSCME's colors from red, white and blue to green, a color he had first associated with the union during a DC 37 organizing drive in the mid-1950s. Green became AFSCME's standard color for three reasons: it is the color that means "go;" it is the color of money; and it is emblematic of springtime, the season of growth and renewal — all points that fit appropriately with the union's attitude as it expanded its membership around the country.

Wurf was committed to placing the union's resources in aggressive organizing campaigns that would take AFSCME into new regions of the country and represent new workers often overlooked by the labor unions of the past. "Wurf had more of a vision of collective bargaining than civil service," Jerry McEntee reflects. "That vision and strategy provided people with the opportunity to build the union. They went together."

Coming out of New York's fractious and politicized environment, Wurf placed a strong emphasis on political organizing as a means to achieve full economic citizenship for America's workers. AFSCME represented more than just a challenge to the status quo of the public sector workplace; its successes could lead to social transformations that would complete the unfinished New Deal, expanding health care and better living conditions for all citizens. To do so, AFSCME had to emulate a traditional, militant trade union.

For the first time in its history, therefore, AFSCME's 1966 Convention resolutions made no mention of civil service, asserting instead a right to collective bargaining. "Even under the best circumstances, even with the most dedicated and competent personnel, even in the greatest absence of political pressures, Civil Service continues to represent unilateralism in labor-management relations in the public service," Wurf stated. His understanding of the role of politics in American life was enhanced by the great upheavals of the 1960s, which showed new social forces organizing for fundamental change in the status of blacks, women, young people and sexual minorities. District Council 33's membership drives of the early 1960s confirmed the soundness of Wurf's emerging national program for AFSCME.

4

In the Political Mix

AFSCME's new emphasis on becoming the strongest voice for working Americans fit well with the views Jerry McEntee had developed in Philadelphia. From an early age, McEntee understood the connection between labor's advancements and its ability to influence the city's formal political power structures. During the early 1960s, McEntee deepened his experience operating within Philadelphia's Democratic Party, which had replaced the G.O.P. as the governing force in urban politics in the post-war period.

In fact, living in the Birdwood Farms section of Northeast Philadelphia, McEntee was becoming a Democratic Party leader. Active in getting out the vote for John F. Kennedy and later Lyndon B. Johnson, and for important local candidates such as U.S. Rep. William J. Green III, he proved his ability to convince people of the importance of the ballot, a skill he would use from then on.

Reflecting on McEntee's love of politics, AFSCME Secretary-Treasurer Lee Saunders recalls, "I was with Jerry in Harrisburg one time, knocking on doors, stopping in at laundromats — and this wasn't what would have been considered one of the best sections of town. Sometimes doors would be slammed on his face, but he knocked on every door. Jerry would never ask anyone to do anything that he hadn't done before or that he wouldn't do now. He makes phone calls at phone banks, he gets his hands dirty, and I think that's what our members like about him. He's not someone sitting on some mountain, he's out there every day of the week."

Such skills were honed during McEntee's years as a Northeast Philadelphia committeeman. That role was crucial to the effectiveness of the party at a neighborhood level. Elected to two-year terms, committeemen were quite literally the local face of the party, the key intermediaries between higher elected officials and citizens, and the people who provided services and made sure the concerns of residents were addressed.

"The party needed committeemen," McEntee recalls, "and I decided to run for that position in the area where I lived." One of the most important functions McEntee would play after his election was overseeing voter registration drives and getting out the vote on Election Day. "I worked hard at being a committeeman. A lot of it back then had to do with making sure that people were registered, Northeast Philadelphia was growing rapidly at the time, and many new people were moving into the area, and I went around and signed them up to vote as Democrats." Seeing him succeed at that task, many fellow Democrats believed Jerry McEntee had the interpersonal skills to advance to ward leader and beyond in the party.

Ward leaders played a vital function in urban politics, especially in determining candidate endorsements. When McEntee first got involved, Babe Devlin, the sister of Congressman Green, was his ward leader, before the election of City Commissioner Maurice Osser to the position. McEntee represented a younger element within Philadelphia's Democratic organization, and many believed he better understood the needs of a new generation. "I ran against Osser for ward leader. I had him nailed, I had the votes. The powers that be at the time — Mayor Jim Tate and his top staff — called me down to city hall."

Mayor Tate was upfront with the young committeeman. "Jerry, we want you to cut this guy a break," he said. "He's old, and he's going to retire soon. We'll get him to tell you that he's going to run this time, but as soon as he is reelected he's going to step down — so at least he'll go out with some pride."

McEntee asked the mayor to give to give him his word that things would play out that way. Tate gave his assurance.

With the promise from the mayor, McEntee spread the word among his supporters that he would not run. Without revealing the exchange he had had with the mayor, he assured them that his time would come soon. The night of the election, however, many still hoped that he would step up and challenge the old ward leader. "Everybody wanted me to run, and it would have been easy to win the position,"

McEntee remembers. "Osser gets nominated, and everybody's looking at me and again, I said no. So he won, but he never retired. That taught me one lesson. Every time you have the damned votes, run with them. Don't give them away."

Even with this chance to become ward leader thwarted, McEntee understood that his position and loyalty to the party would open up a range of other possibilities. "Northeast Philadelphia's population was booming by the mid-1960s, and there was a new legislative seat being created, and Mayor Tate offered me that," McEntee recalls. "I turned it down. By that point, I had decided to stick with the union. Instead Steve Wojack ran, and he became a good friend of mine."

The experience in Philadelphia's political world was crucial to McEntee's development and worldview, and reinforced his understanding of his position within AFSCME. "Being a committeeman showed me how to organize, how to talk to people," McEntee stated. "That was where I found out that I had some skills."

The connection between political effectiveness and labor's advancement was one of the important lessons of these years. In 1967, Philadelphia's political scene grew fractious, as the city's Democratic Committee chairman, former Congressman Frank Smith, announced that he would not support incumbent Mayor Tate for a second term. Instead, Smith came out for Alexander Hemphill, a challenger from the city's elite Chestnut Hill section.

With the city's ward leaders divided, and with limited access to the Democratic Party's resources, Tate refused to back down, turning to organized labor — always his strongest base within the city's vast blue-collar neighborhoods — for support. With much at stake in the race, AFSCME District Council 33 mobilized its members to campaign for the mayor, whose strong personal relationship with the union leadership proved an important factor in mediating the problems of the municipal workplace.

McEntee oversaw important aspects of the Tate campaign and helped with fundraising. Meeting with Tate at a downtown Philadelphia hotel, he said, "We'll be good friends when you win.'"

With solid backing from AFSCME and other unions across the city, Mayor Tate beat Hemphill in the Democratic primary and went on to defeat Philadelphia District Attorney Arlen Specter in the November election. Tate, who had always been a strong friend of labor, never forgot the support he received from DC 33. McEntee's view of his alliance with Tate, "It was a deal, as most things are, a deal."

5

The Young Organizer

In the midst of the 1967 mayoral race, Jerry McEntee decided the time was right for a more aggressive organizing approach. Sections of Philadelphia's municipal services still did not have union representation, and a wide range of non-profit sector workplaces needed representation that AFSCME could deliver.

At this point, an important figure joined in planning AFSCME's organizing drives in Philadelphia: James Hogwood, a sanitation truck driver from Philadelphia's Germantown section. Representing a new generation of African-American workers in the city service, Hogwood had been instrumental in putting together a coalition that eventually replaced Bill McEntee as business agent of Sanitation Local 427 in 1965. Despite the fact that Hogwood had led a faction opposed to his father, McEntee and Hogwood became close friends, and enjoyed a long association that lasted until Hogwood's death in the early 1980s.

The partnership between Jerry McEntee and James Hogwood brought a surge of new members into AFSCME's Philadelphia chapter. Their friendship and their effectiveness as organizers became legendary in Council 33 and in the AFSCME International offices. "I remember I'd go out to try to organize new members with Hogwood. Jimmy was about six-foot-five, 250 pounds with a shaved head, a real tough-looking guy," McEntee said years later.

Among the first groups the team organized were municipal workers and school district employees in Easton, Pennsylvania. With those gains in hand, McEntee and Hogwood considered making connections with city workers in other mid-sized Pennsylvania municipalities, including Lebanon, well known as the producer of baloney lunchmeat. "People would see a black man like Jimmy and a smaller white guy like me walking down the street together," McEntee recalls, "and didn't know what to do, what to make of us. I don't think we ever did organize a soul in Lebanon."

McEntee's and Hogwood's attempts at organizing did bear fruit in those years — several thousand new members for AFSCME between 1966 and 1970. The organizing of over 700 women school crossing guards was Council 33's most successful membership drive of the period. Women made up a growing section of AFSCME's membership across the United States, reflecting the increasing numbers of women working in clerical positions as well as in social work and service and technical positions in institutions of higher education.

One group that had long been overlooked remained the thousands of women across the nation who worked as school crossing guards. The demand for those guards had expanded to unprecedented levels in the early 1950s, as the millions of baby-boom children started elementary school. Across the nation, women took these part time jobs in an effort to allow police officers — the ones who traditionally had taken up these duties — to take on other services. Philadelphia's crossing guard program had proved a model for similar programs in big cities across the United States.

While parents appreciated the service women provided as crossing guards, such part-time positions were not well paid. Many of these women — some of whom had been iconic Rosie the Riveters in the nation's war plants of the 1940s, frequently from union families — demanded better pay. With initial 1952 wages set at four dollars a day, the women sought pay increases almost immediately, forming the Crossing Guards Association in early 1954. The group petitioned Police Commissioner Thomas J. Gibbons with a four-point program requesting an extra two dollars a day, payment for school holidays, health and accident insurance, and summer employment as guards at city recreation centers. Although such appeals had considerable support from the public, the Crossing Guard Association had no success in achieving their stated goals.

Although crossing guards were assigned to their own neighborhoods, the women exhibited a spirit of association that united them into a sisterhood manifested in numerous meetings and luncheons where guards could gather with others from across the city. One group formed the Guardettes, a chorus that entertained at annual benefits, hospitals and police department socials throughout the year.

Despite their popularity with city residents and the children they protected, crossing guards in 1962 were still working at wages little better than they had made ten years before. In addition, women complained that their uniforms — heavy black overcoats with brass buttons and military styled hats with the seal of the City of Philadelphia — had to be purchased, cleaned and maintained out of their own pockets. Repeated attempts at gaining the support of police department officials received little more than patronizing comments or silence.

Faced with continuing frustration in their appeals to city officials, several women contacted District Council 33 in early 1967 to see about affiliation. At the first organizing meeting in May 1967, McEntee and Hogwood were amazed to see 680 women show up, enthusiastic in their support of a union. "Coming to the meeting, even before we got to the doors, we could hear the excitement in that room, the decibels were up to the ceiling, it was so loud!" With almost no opposition from city officials, and with substantial support from the public, the crossing guard campaign was one of the swiftest in Council 33's history.

In the days following this initial meeting, Jerry McEntee phoned Police Commissioner Frank L. Rizzo to request that he give his approval to the women's campaign. Rizzo responded positively, stating that he had many friends among the guards and always believed they were an important section of the police department that needed wage increases and better treatment. The negotiation process with the City of Philadelphia was almost as quick as the organizing drive: by November, the crossing guards' negotiating team had signed their first contract, establishing higher wages, health and welfare benefits, compensation for days lost to inclement weather and holidays. In honor of the support the women had received from Jerry McEntee through the year, the guards chose 1956 — the year he had graduated from college — as the new local's number.

The 700 members of Philadelphia's crossing guard's union formed District Council 33's largest section of women, adding to the diversity represented under AFSCME's broadening tent. McEntee never forgot the women of Local 1956. For decades into the future, he would demonstrate a commitment to the advancement of women within AFSCME and the labor movement and also throughout society.

On the heels of the crossing-guard campaign, McEntee and Hogwood initiated a separate drive at one of the city's most cherished institutions, the Philadelphia Zoo. First established in 1869 as one of the nation's first zoological gardens, the zoo was often overlooked as a possible place for unionization, despite the fact that several hundred employees there performed maintenance, custodial and concession duties — not to mention providing for the upkeep and health of the animals. Looking to the zoo as a place for AFSCME to represent its workers again underscores the new attitude it was bringing to worker representation.

The origins of the zoo organizing drive date from a survey McEntee and Hogwood did of the city's unorganized public venues, looking for places to organize "We went to the planetarium at the Franklin Institute, Philadelphia's famous science museum out on the Parkway," McEntee says. "They had maintenance workers, tour guides and administrators, and we went in to see if we could bring them into the district council. In the dark planetarium, with the planets and comets going all around, we fell sound asleep! We went there every day and fell asleep.

"So we walked out to the zoo. I think it was like a dime to get in. The first place we go is the tiger place, where you could see all the tigers were roaming around. There was a guy cleaning up in one of these areas, and I called him over, 'Hey, bud, come here a minute.... You got a union here? Anybody who represents you, or speaks out for you?'

"'No, I wouldn't call it a union. But the guy down at the birdhouse is in charge of us all. Not as our employer, but he's the closest thing we have to a spokesperson.'

"So Jimmy and I went down to the elephant house. They had these workers there shoveling up these big turds from the elephants. It smelled bad. Same question and the same response: "'Go see the guy in the birdhouse.'

"We go down to the birdhouse and there's nobody down there in that birdhouse but birds," McEntee recalls. "We're looking all over for someone to talk to, and finally a guy comes out of the back. It's Eddie Keller — he's the one in charge of the birdhouse. I try to get him interested in AFSCME, and right away, he is. Eddie's from the Fairmount section, a pretty pro-union area, and he's plugged in to the idea."

Although neither knew it at the time, this was the first meeting of a friendship that endures to this day — and would have a great impact on the history of AFSCME in Pennsylvania and elsewhere.

Eddie Keller started at the zoo in 1963 at the age of 21, after working a couple of years as a stock boy at the Strawbridge & Clothier department store. Keller noted that it was "run by the Zoological Society of Philadelphia, which was kind of the blue bloods of the city. It was kind of philanthropic. The zoo was set up on a trust where these wealthy folks had endowments for the zoo, while the city provided a capital budget for major improvements and displays."

Keller told McEntee and Hogwood about the brief history of unionization there. In 1965, the Teamsters attempted to organize, promising better wages and treatment. The son of a Philadelphia truck driver and Teamster member, Keller signed up right away. Zoo management sought to usurp the union cause by establishing an independent association, the Zoo Employees Independent Union. While clearly an in-house, management-controlled set up, the ZEIU was given a contract establishing an immediate 20 cents an hour raise, with an additional five cents an hour the second and third year.

Although Keller would have preferred to stay with the Teamsters, he accepted the members' request that he serve as president of the in-house organization. Even with the new labor-management relationship, little changed for the zoo's employees. Besides the low pay, the zoo was open almost every day, including every major holiday. Only those few employees with over 30 years of service could have days off — half a day Saturday and all day Sunday.

Such treatment was beginning to change at some of the larger zoos around the country. As he began planning an organizing drive, Jerry McEntee researched conditions at the Bronx Zoo and other similar institutions around the country that AFSCME represented. Under DC 37's contracts, New York zoo workers had higher wages, regular raises, pensions, sick days and holidays.

Believing that they could quickly enlist the majority of workers at the Philadelphia Zoo, McEntee and Hogwood went to see the institution's director. McEntee remembers the head man as "dressed in big leather boots up to his knees, wearing a kind of pith helmet and a gun in a holster, along with a long whip in his belt. I guess he thought the animals were going to break out."

The exchange went like this:

McEntee: "The people who work here want to join a union."

The director: "Yeah, I know, they're in a union."

McEntee: "I know they're in a union. But they don't like that union."

The director: "We even got a kind of contract. What are we going to do?"

McEntee: "Well, you better do something, or this place is going to be screwed up. I'll tell you what we'll do. You agree to have an election, and we'll see what union they pick. If they pick AFSCME, we'll do the same contract."

The director: "Okay, that's a deal."

An election overseen by the American Arbitration Association was scheduled almost immediately, and AFSCME won by an overwhelming margin — 109-17. AFSCME chartered the section as Local 752.

The day the vote result was declared, McEntee went again to meet with the director of the zoo, and informed him that AFSCME had won the election, as he had predicted. Jerry told him, "That's the good news. The not so good news is this: that contract's no good."

The director stared at him, baffled. "Wait, you said you'd accept it."

"I accept it, but those people don't accept it," McEntee explained. "That's why they voted for us — to get out of that.... So you've got to negotiate a new contract."

"That summer was one of the best I ever had," McEntee recalls. "I sat out under a tree at the zoo, negotiating the contract. He said the zoo didn't have any money, and I said raise the entrance fee to 50 cents. He said no one would come. I said raise it to 50 cents and see. So he raised it to 50 cents, and the exact same number of people came. Even with that change, we still didn't have enough money to help these workers. I went over to talk to Mayor Tate. I said, 'Look at these poor souls over there at the zoo. We want them to have the same pay classification as similar employees who work for the city, to make the same amount of money.'"

Ed Keller was involved in these sessions, and recalled the important role that Tate's labor advisor Harry Gelfand played in these meetings. McEntee continued, "He took a look and agreed to do it. We got these people so much damned money it was absurd. I still remember the printer. His name was Tommy Riggins. We got him a $5,000 raise, because the printer at the city got that much a year."

Even with this, the zoo workers came close to striking. All of the members of the bargaining unit got called down to DC 33 headquarters at Juniper and Arch Streets in downtown Philadelphia to vote on the contract: either accept it, or go out on strike. As McEntee recalls it, "All of our people from the zoo were at a bar across the street from the union offices, and by the time we brought back the contract, many of them had one drink too many. They were yelling, 'No contract! Let's strike!' Even Tommy Riggins, the zoo printer who had gotten the colossal raise, joined in this chorus. I finally got up there and screamed at them, yelling that they had to accept the contact, and they listened, they finally voted the contract in."

Other organizing drives of this era were important to Jerry McEntee's understanding of effective worker outreach.

Some organizing drives failed, including one to represent several thousand cafeteria employees in Philadelphia's public schools. But others succeeded, resulting, for example, in new locals representing cafeteria workers and library staff at the University of Pennsylvania. These early campaigns would provide valuable experience that he would eventually draw upon when he initiated one of the most ambitious union organizing drives in American history: the Commonwealth of Pennsylvania. All of these successes between 1958 and 1973 secured McEntee's position in American labor history as one of the movement's most successful organizers.

Reflecting on what it takes to be a good union organizer, McEntee says, "You have to have it in your guts. You have to be ready and able to work hard. You have to believe in it. It's hard work, but it's also a hell of a lot of fun."

6

Memphis 1968

McEntee's leadership in organizing AFSCME in Philadelphia was part of the new spirit of union growth emerging across the country. An important part of this was AFSCME's efforts to organize in the southern states. Despite some AFSCME presence, the South had resisted public sector unionization as vehemently as it had unions in the private sphere. Since the 1930s, AFSCME locals in the South rarely had gained official recognition, and they sought moderate shifts in civil service improvements. Conditions for many southern municipal workers were among the worst in the United States.

Sanitation workers are an essential part of AFSCME's history. The original nucleus of many of the union's urban councils, sanitation workers represented a paradox in the American imagination. While undeniably strong individuals doing difficult physical labor few other men could do, they were also among the lowest paid in the urban economy. No one would deny the social necessity of what these men did; without it, modern society could not long function. Yet to many citizens, they remained outside the pale of social acceptance, and were considered social pariahs by some.

These conditions existed for sanitation workers throughout the United States. In the 20th century, as increasing numbers of African-American migrants began new lives in the urban North, thousands found positions in municipal labor jobs, mostly in lifting and dumping a city's rubbish, garbage and coal ash. In the South, however, the terms of this labor seemed unchangeable, with black men occupying the lowest jobs and unable to advance into driving or mechanical positions.

While sometimes lauded as more progressive than other southern cities, Memphis exemplified that situation. Recalling the types of work he did on a Memphis trash route, T.O. Jones recalled the particular hardship of carrying 50-gallon drums filled with rubbish from homeowners' yards to the curb. "You carried those tubs on your head and shoulders. Most of those tubs were leaking, and that stuff was falling all over you. You got home; you had to take your clothes off at the door because you didn't want to bring all that filth in the house. We didn't have a place to eat lunch. You didn't have a place to use the restroom. Conditions were just horrible.

"We didn't have any say about nothing. Whatever they said, that's what you had to do: right, wrong or indifferent. Anything that you did that the supervisor didn't like, he'd fire you, whatever. You didn't have recourse, a way of getting back at him. We just got tired of all that."

In the 1960s, the only types of municipal employment available to blacks were in harsh trash removal or sewage treatment positions. City services were racially segregated, with the Memphis Police Department remaining a lilywhite bastion. Accounts of police brutality had long made up a part of the history of black residents, with increasing reports of intimidation and abuse surfacing in 1967. As in other southern cities in the early 1960s, Memphis sanitation workers resisted their treatment on the job and as citizens. In response, city sanitation managers fired all workers known to support their union. Following the death of two men who had been crushed when the hydraulic plates of a sanitation truck malfunctioned in early 1968, workers demanded that city managers accept AFSCME Local 1733 as their bargaining agent. Bolstered by white support, Mayor Henry Loeb refused to meet these demands. Calling for recognition and dues check-offs, strikers and their allies picketed and marched as strikebreakers replaced them on the routes.

In the face of this struggle, the Memphis sanitation workers called on Dr. Martin Luther King Jr. for his support. Dr. King often spoke of the links between the struggle for workers' rights and the cause of civil rights. "The coalition that can have the greatest impact in the struggle for human dignity here in America is that of the Negro and the forces of labor, because their fortunes are so closely intertwined," he wrote in 1962. He knew that the labor movement had been at the forefront of social and economic progress in the United States, and he wanted to harness the power of working people to transform America into a more just and prosperous society.

With Dr. King's organization already in the midst of organizing a national Poor People's march that summer, his key advisors urged him to stay out of the developing conflict in Tennessee. He accepted the invitation however, seeing the plight of the sanitation workers and their families as part of the broader struggle facing Americans who faced injustice and economic fears. On three occasions in 1968, he traveled to Memphis to stand with the sanitation workers of AFSCME Local 1733.

On the night before he was assassinated at the Lorraine Motel, Dr. King addressed the AFSCME sanitation workers at the Mason Temple in Memphis. "You are demanding that this city will respect the dignity of labor," he declared. "So often we overlook the worth and significance of those who are not in the professional jobs, in the so-called big jobs, but let me say to you tonight that whenever you are engaged in work that serves humanity, for the building of humanity, it has dignity and it has worth."

He continued: "Let us rise up tonight with a greater readiness. Let us stand with a greater determination. And let us move on in these powerful days, these days of challenge, to make America what it ought to be. We have an opportunity to make America a better nation."

More than four decades after the strike, McEntee would note: "AFSCME is still fighting for better lives for the working families of Memphis, and we are still committed to Dr. King's dream for our nation and the world."

7

Driving AFSCME to the Forefront

By the end of the decade, AFSCME's members and labor experts saw no reason why the union would not continue to grow to astronomical numbers. In 1968, Wurf announced "We shall be bigger than the Teamsters, bigger than the Autoworkers, or the Steelworkers or the Machinists. If we meet our challenge, AFSCME can be the Number One union in all America." Wurf's dreams of a larger, more dynamic union were not unfounded. AFSCME was bringing in more than 1,000 members a week by the end of the decade, going from 19th largest to the sixth largest union within the AFL-CIO in less than five years. By 1970, AFSCME was negotiating more than one thousand collective bargaining agreements around the country. The union's potential for continued growth through the decade seemed beyond dispute. So did its potential as force in American society.

Not all of AFSCME's organizing efforts hit gold. In one important drive, Wurf sent an army of organizers to New York State in an attempt to bring in tens of thousands of state employees. Despite great promise and interest among many of these workers, the New York organizing efforts came up short, as workers chose to stick with an independent civil service association. At a cost of millions of dollars in resources, the New York drive was a major setback.

In his bones, McEntee knew himself to be a labor organizer; and with his organizing drives in the Philadelphia area seemingly maxed out, he looked for other areas to mobilize. With his deep connections in Philadelphia and Pennsylvania politics, McEntee considered the possibility of launching a similarly ambitious organizing drive in the entire Keystone State. In 1967, Pennsylvania firefighters and police officers began pressing for legislation that would grant them the right to organize and bargain for wages and working conditions, something that existing laws forbade. McEntee believed it was time to press for similar legal openings for the commonwealth employees who worked in labor, maintenance, clerical and professional categories — an enormous section of unorganized workers across the state.

"I knew that the state employees should be the target," McEntee recalls, "because they worked under a single employer, and because of their sheer size." AFSCME did have a presence in the commonwealth already, strong in Philadelphia and weak in other regions. Pennsylvania's existing section of state employees, AFSCME Council 26, traced its roots back to 1938, but had little to show for its activities; by the end of the 1960s it had no more than two thousand dues paying members.

Another AFSCME section, Council 60 in Pittsburgh, represented fewer than 4,000 members scattered across a series of school districts, courts and cities and townships. Other small units had also affiliated with AFSCME in the early 1960s, with a local of city workers in Johnstown and Altoona, and a few fledgling sections in some of the state's hospitals. In a Philadelphia suburb, a core group had sought AFSCME representation in a Pennsylvania state office building. Overall, however, Pennsylvania remained outside AFSCME's reach.

The situation in Pennsylvania seemed open to change by the end of the 1960s. McEntee had begun to give the union a wedge in certain sections of the state. AFSCME had gained recognition of two city locals in Easton, and had added municipal workers and school district employees in Lancaster. The most promising strategy, he believed, would be an all-out effort to sign up the more than 103,000 state employees across the entire commonwealth. Most others did not believe such a grand strategy feasible, and he understood the reasons for their skepticism:

"There was no way to organize the state workers unless we had some kind of recognition, with some kind of collective bargaining rights. You could go someplace with that. We didn't have any of these kinds of things, but we started to organize the state employees anyway," McEntee recalls.

There had been dreams of organizing across the commonwealth before, but none had been realized. Pennsylvania seemed like a natural base for bringing public workers into the House of Labor. It had a strong and militant tradition of labor unions and was home to some of the most powerful unions in the nation, including the Steelworkers and Miners. They were powerful forces in both their industries and in state politics. But organizing public workers had always been another matter.

People from Council 33, including his father, were on the Pennsylvania State Labor Federation. They would attend federation meetings, McEntee says, "and always at the end they would bring up that they wanted to get legislation to get collective bargaining rights for public workers across the commonwealth. It was always the last item on the agenda, and it never really got handled. That took a real long while, but then things began to develop."

Some AFSCME organizers had done some organizing in the state hospitals, prison facilities and maintenance yards before the 1960s, but there was little to show for it. In 1969, McEntee began looking into some of those earlier drives, including those at Polk Hospital in Western Pennsylvania. "I went up to Polk and asked around. At the time, it didn't go anywhere, but it built a foundation. Then we went to other places: to Warren, a geriatric hospital; to Harrisburg State Hospital. We did very well at Harrisburg: it was one of the first, probably the first, where we had 400 members, which was the largest membership in the Commonwealth outside Philadelphia."

Economic conditions of the time made the going tough. The pay for state employees was low, the working conditions were poor. But that provided fertile ground for organizing. One group, in Pittsburgh, as McEntee recalls it, "couldn't get dues deduction, but because things were so bad, they had a lot of people. They even had a couple of strikes. Things were acting up around the state. In Easton, we must have had five strikes there and we didn't even have the union recognized. We also had a group of pretty militant workers at Byberry State Mental Hospital in the Far Northeastern section of Philadelphia. They used to meet in the basement of my house." Conversations with the host went like this:

Workers: "Can we come up and meet with you, Jerry?"

McEntee: "Sure, come on up."

Workers: "We're going on strike tomorrow morning."

McEntee: "Oh, really, are you? You're not allowed. It's against state law."

Workers: "Oh, that's okay, we're going to anyway. Will you lead it?"

McEntee: "Sure. I don't work there, but I'll lead it."

One of those discussions, McEntee recalls, ended memorably: "Everybody was going to meet at the Byberry Hospital chapel at 3:30 a.m. I heard we were ready to go out, to close it down. The strike's called. I go to the chapel, nobody's there. Nobody got to the chapel on time. The reason was that management had heard about the strike meeting, and in an effort to stop it, had given all of the workers overtime. They worked the overtime, and they never went on strike. Management was pretty smart in that one."

From these early meetings with isolated sections of workers around the state, McEntee realized the time was ripe to coordinate a more substantial organizing campaign. Pay for state workers was abysmal, with many men and women taking home a paltry $2,700 a year after taxes. All workers faced "macing," in which they were expected to provide the party in power a cash "contribution" for campaign coffers; all knew that failure to provide this "voluntary assessment" would be to lose their jobs. Even worse was an abusive patronage system that ran rampant across the state, with workers facing the severe logic of the spoils system that surfaced each election cycle: winning politicians rewarded party loyalists and supporters while dismissing all existing employees, regardless of their job performance. Bernard "Buck" Martin, the first AFSCME organizer assigned to help McEntee, recalls that "Thousands of jobs depended on election success. Jaded taxpayers silently condoned this system."

An encouraging sign for labor and motivating development for AFSCME was the growing support Pennsylvania state troopers were gathering as they pushed for bargaining rights. Riding a wave of popular support, uniformed personnel proposed them as amendments to Pennsylvania law in 1967, and Act 111 passed one year later. In McEntee's estimation, the success of this bill marked a turning point in Pennsylvania history. And with growing support in polls for the rights of public employees, he saw a golden moment for AFSCME;

a similar bill for non-uniformed personnel, he felt, could pass in Harrisburg.

Pennsylvania's position within the broader national history of this period factored into his view. In his history of Council 13, Carmen Brutto observes that the political shifts after 1964 gave rise to a more moderate form of liberal Republicanism. Following the overwhelming defeat of Barry Goldwater in 1964, many moderate Republicans believed that the future success of the party lay not in right-wing extremism, which had been resoundingly rejected by the American people, but in a policy agenda that embraced some forms of social legislation while maintaining commitments to fiscal limits.

National political figures such as New York's Nelson Rockefeller and Pennsylvania's Hugh Scott were liberal Republicans who also embraced civil rights and were often open to pro-labor measures. In 1966, Republican Lieutenant Governor Raymond P. Shafer was elected governor on a moderate platform. Soon after his election, Shafer supported a constitutional change to allow arbitration binding on government bodies, as well as the right of uniformed public employees to collective bargaining. The passing of Act III also revealed a growing tolerance among Pennsylvanians for public employee unions.

Understanding the historical significance of these revisions to the state's labor laws, McEntee coordinated a major campaign to revise the 1947 Public Employee Law of Pennsylvania to extend similar rights to all commonwealth employees. Building support with other labor unions and with a range of community organizations, which helped lobby for labor reform through letters and phone calls to politicians across the state, McEntee succeeded in crafting a bill that applied to workers who would be in AFSCME's jurisdiction.

Governor Shafer formed the Commission to Revise the Public Employee Law of Pennsylvania, which consisted of twelve members who conducted hearings with state workers and investigated the current law's impact on workplace conditions. The commission concluded that the existing state law restricting collective bargaining was "unreasonable and unenforceable" and suggested a new law that would guarantee the rights of public employees to bargain with state officials.

"When these proposals were announced, I knew that a new day had come for public workers in Pennsylvania," McEntee says.

The 1969 committee report led pro-union legislators in Harrisburg to craft a house bill that proposed the overturn of existing public employee laws. McEntee channeled AFSCME's resources into a continuation of the public relations campaign he had begun earlier in the year, raising the awareness of the bill's importance across the state. On July 23, 1970, the bill was passed as Act 195. It became law in October 1970, making Pennsylvania one of the first states in the nation to allow public sector negotiations. Realizing that this political measure now opened up the possibility for a more substantial organizing drive, McEntee called for an all-out campaign by AFSCME.

8

Tackling Pennsylvania

Many years later, it is often assumed that McEntee's victory in changing Pennsylvania labor law — the realization of a goal first envisioned by the state's labor leaders more than thirty years earlier — was immediately understood by AFSCME International leadership as an opening for massive state organizing. At the time, however, a campaign of that magnitude posed serious challenges to AFSCME's finances, and many balked at such boldness. The first step in the new venture was to convince Jerry Wurf that it was feasible.

"Jerry was a great organizer, and he had balls," McEntee recalls. The Philadelphian thus believed that ultimately, Wurf would give his approval for the ambitious actions he had in mind. The two agreed to meet in Washington. It was the summer of 1970. McEntee remembers his preparation for the meeting: "I went to a map store and bought a great big map of Pennsylvania. Then I did some research so I could put on the map all the highway yards along with the approximate amount of people that worked at them. I did this for all the jobsites throughout Pennsylvania. And I did the same thing for all of the state office buildings."

Wurf had been tipped off that McEntee had a big proposal ready for the meeting. When McEntee came into his office, he asked him up front:

Wurf: "Well, what do you want to do?"

McEntee: "Organize the Pennsylvania state employees."

Wurf: "Which state employees?"

McEntee: "All of them."

Wurf: "Ah, that's bull. I just came off a losing campaign in the state of New York, and we just got rubbed all over the place."

McEntee pressed on. He spread his map out on Wurf's table and said, "If you make that kind of investment in Pennsylvania, we'll end up with thousands and thousands of members and workers."

Wurf wasn't against organizing workers in Pennsylvania; his disagreement with McEntee was more a question of strategy. Based on his recent setback in New York, Wurf believed that a more cautious approach was needed — going after specific municipalities and regions, rather than an all-out campaign covering the entire state. He was also concerned that, once

AFSCME began, other unions would also campaign to organize Pennsylvania's workers.

McEntee was emphatic that whatever union competition emerged, AFSCME could win. "Look, I'm telling you, we can wipe them out. If you go with me and roll some dice, we can blow them away, all of them." Finally, the young organizer's enthusiasm convinced Wurf. "All right, all right," he said. "I'll roll the dice with you. You put it together, and let's go after all of it. I'm ready to make the investment."

Years later, Jerry McEntee remembers this meeting as a pivotal moment in both in his career and AFSCME's history, one that set the stage nationally for the union — by 1980 — to reach a membership of more than one million. "I admired Jerry's willingness to take that shot," McEntee says. "Here I was, just after what happened in New York, asking him for something like two million dollars to run a Pennsylvania campaign."

As it has throughout AFSCME's history, politics and the potential for organizing went hand in hand. The beginning of AFSCME's Keystone State effort coincided with the state's 1970 gubernatorial race, which pundits believed would be close. This contest would figure strongly in how the organizing campaign played out, and McEntee paid close attention to how it developed through its early stages. By early 1970, as lobbying for Act 195 reached full throttle, it became clear that Milton Shapp, a pro-labor Philadelphia businessman, would be the Democratic challenger to Republican Raymond Broderick.

McEntee recalls: "I called Shapp and told him that we would endorse him, support him. I got DC 33 and other people to do the same. Shapp let everyone know that he would be in favor of collective bargaining for public employees. When he won, it was common knowledge that he was going to allow public employee unions in Pennsylvania."

One clear indication that Shapp represented a change in labor-management policy was his emphasis on introducing workplace standards that were by then common in private-sector workplaces across the nation. In place of party henchmen in personnel management, Shapp appointed professionally trained experts in labor-management procedures. McEntee recalls this policy change. "Ernie Kline was the lieutenant governor, and he started to gear up for having unions — hiring personnel officers — doing those kinds of things. I met with Chris Zervanos who had become the personnel director for Pennsylvania, and we talked about establishing bargaining units and other types of things, which nobody even understood what it meant. He advised Shapp that to initiate unionization elections, the state would establish professional bargaining units, from trades and labor, institutional sections, and technical so it made some sense about it. Then we started organizing the workers."

After McEntee's meeting with Wurf, the International disbanded Council 26 and replaced it with the Pennsylvania Organizing Committee. Appointed the POC's director, McEntee ran operations with just one staff member — Buck Martin — during the first weeks of the campaign.

Remembering when he met the young organizer from Philadelphia, Martin recalls, "I first met with McEntee at the Allegheny Hotel, near the Pittsburgh airport, in August 1969. He was the area director for Pennsylvania, and I was the staff. Jerry spread that map on the hotel room's bed. It was color-coordinated with pins marking all the state facilities. Every highway garage, every welfare hospital, park site, university and prison had its own pin. Departments were also designated by color; and sites that had large numbers of workers were also shown. Jerry asked me to coordinate the western half of the state — 34 counties. He took the rest."

McEntee told Martin that he believed that it would take about five years for them to organize all of the state workers. To handle this massive task — one of the largest organizing drives in U.S. labor history — McEntee convinced AFSCME to bolster his staff. In early 1970, several of McEntee's Philadelphia associates, including Pasquale "Pat" Salvatore, from DC 33's correctional officers' local, Ed Keller and Local 1510's President Mario DiFurio, joined the drive.

The first foray was daunting, even for McEntee, who had grown used to organizing setbacks. "The first meeting of state employees we called was at Ebensburg Center, a state school and hospital for patients with intellectual disabilities outside Johnstown. We leafleted all the entrances and held the meeting across the street. Seven people came to that meeting — seven people who didn't want their names used, seven people who said, 'I'm not really here' or 'Pretend I'm not here.' When we saw the fantastic element of fear in these people, we knew we had our work cut out for us."

Even with the apprehension many Pennsylvania workers felt about being identified with the unionization drive, some emerged as leaders and became legends in AFSCME. One of the founding mothers of what would become Council 13 was Wanda Weaver, a clerical worker with the Pennsylvania Department of Transportation. Believing that she and her fellow workers needed union protection, Weaver stopped in at AFSCME's offices in Harrisburg one day during her lunch break. Introduced to Jerry McEntee, she told him she could help organize in her building.

McEntee handed her a two-inch thick stack of green union cards. Recalled Weaver in a 1997 interview, "The next day, McEntee's mouth fell open large enough to ride a horse into when I handed over those completed cards." Through her continued support of the organizing drive across the city, Weaver helped establish Local 2534 and Council 90, and later helped to form the council's first women's committee.

These initial months of the campaign, while exhausting, also continued to develop the strong friendship between McEntee and Ed Keller, who was to follow McEntee as executive director of Council 13. They still share stories of those early days, many of them spent on the road. They drove a truck used by the Maritime Union in organizing drives, with that union's logo on the side. "We were coming home on a Saturday, after a tough week," says McEntee, "and the truck conked out, of all places, right in front of Byberry Hospital. We were able to chug along, hitting the gas pedal, and we finally pulled into the Byberry parking lot and parked the truck and left it there. Some patients probably drove away in it."

Other humorous stories also color this moment of McEntee's life as an organizer. "I went out to Woodhaven hospital to organize the workers there. I went in at lunchtime, and there were dozens of people there eating their lunches, mostly carpenters and plumbers, who in many ways should be the easiest to organize in an institutional setting like that. I was up there giving a forceful speech, really wailing about what AFSCME was going to get for them, and I could see everybody shaking their heads, especially these guys who were standing in the back. I finished the speech and got down and said, 'All right, we are going to start passing around cards for you to sign to join the union.'

"I said to a guy standing next to me, 'Wow, I did good, man. Did you see all those guys in the back shaking their heads in agreement with me?'

"He said, 'Yeah, they're the patients!'"

As the AFSCME worker-outreach efforts gained ground, other unions, as McEntee had expected, also began organizing to sign up thousands of potential members. McEntee devised a strategy to build a statewide union. Ed Keller notes that "McEntee knew exactly what he wanted." When AFSCME sought certification as the exclusive bargaining agent for two units, the state maintenance and trade workers, and first-line supervisors, the Teamsters and, more formidably, a combined organization of operating engineers and the laborers union known as PennEl, mounted competing efforts. But AFSCME prevailed.

Says McEntee of those early contests with other unions, "Originally, we were the only ones around, but when we got collective bargaining, other unions started flying in like vampires. We beat them all. In every damned election that came down the pike, AFSCME came out on top."

The fact that other unions sought to represent workers within AFSCME's jurisdiction speaks to the uncharted nature of public sector unionization on the eve of the 1970s. During the organizing campaign, McEntee met with Wendell W. Young III, the leader of the Philadelphia-based Retail Clerks International Association Local 1357, which represented 10,000 supermarket and department store clerks in southeastern Pennsylvania. Young, who also came out of the political world of Philadelphia and had close ties with AFSCME Council 33, asked McEntee for jurisdiction over the four thousand clerks who worked in the state-controlled liquor stores.

"I'll gamble with you," McEntee said. "You can have the clerks if they're voting as a separate unit; but if they're part of the larger, white-collar clerical unit, we're going to take them. We can't split them off."

Young agreed, and promised to lobby hard for passage of Act 195. Unexpectedly, however, Retail Clerks Local 1357 eventually gained exclusive rights to represent Pennsylvania's liquor clerks the following year. Politics explains that shift: Young served as the lead officer on the Labor for Shapp committee, which proved crucial in mobilizing thousands of unionists across the state to come out for the Democrats in 1970; in recognition of Young's work, Shapp agreed to split the liquor clerks off from the office workers as a favor. Despite their competition in this campaign, McEntee and Young worked together on political campaigns over the next forty years and remain close friends.

In the first few weeks of Milton Shapp's administration, McEntee faced another unexpected development. Despite Shapp's promise that he would not adhere to the old standards of the spoils system, several hundred laborers in the state Department of Transportation received pink slips in early 1971. Fears of wholesale job cuts had motivated many workers to sign union cards with AFSCME in the weeks leading up to the November 1970 election. Indeed, realizing the potential consequences of a Democratic win, Republican county chairmen across the state urged all registered with the party to join the union in order to protect their jobs. According to AFSCME organizer Donald Cutler, "it didn't make any difference to us who they were, and at that time they happened to be Republicans. We wanted to save their jobs, to nail down their security once and for all. We told them what the unions could do about security, and we went from county to county to put together a campaign that could sustain itself and win elections."

Hearing of the firings, a furious McEntee asked Wurf to join him in putting pressure on Shapp to reverse his order. Wurf immediately drove to Harrisburg to join McEntee in a meeting with Shapp at the governor's mansion. Shapp justified the layoffs by saying, "Hey, you know, these people are all Republican leaders."

"What, are you crazy?" Wurf responded. "We're talking about a guy who drives a truck in Bedford County or a flagman in Columbus County, and if you are going to tell us they are the real leaders of the Republican Party, you are pulling our leg. Policy makers that work for the state, that's different. You do what you want with policy makers and top-level administrators. But you are talking about the rank-and-file worker who has nothing to do with policy. It's our union's mission to protect them, and protect them we're going to do."

Shapp said he'd think about it, and asked them to return the following day. When they did, they were met by a junior assistant who said the governor was not available.

Enraged by this insult, McEntee and Wurf left the meeting. In an official press statement, the former declared, "Depriving working men of jobs for the crime of belonging to the wrong political party is an indecent act." He promised to fight for those who had been let go, and immediately sought an injunction against the governor's actions. The case made its way through the courts, gaining media attention across the commonwealth.

In unprecedented actions, McEntee organized hundreds of workers to testify before court officers about their treatment on the job and the ways that the political patronage system brought havoc to their lives. After repeated appeals, the case eventually went before the Pennsylvania Supreme Court, which in May 1971 overturned Shapp's decision, ordering that more than 1,500 workers be rehired. McEntee's stand had proven one important principle: that AFSCME was a fighting organization, willing to overturn years of political tradition in order to protect workers' interest — regardless of party affiliation.

AFSCME's successful challenge to Pennsylvania's existing political culture — which dated as far back as the days of Andrew Jackson — altered the basic power structure and improved conditions for workers for years to come. All subsequent AFSCME contracts in Pennsylvania and elsewhere spelled out that workers could not be discriminated against based upon "race, creed, color, sex, age, national origin, union membership or political affiliation."

McEntee's fight against patronage also shifted the meaning of state employment — away from political favor granted as an award for political support toward a notion of life-long career service and professionalism. In this way, his Pennsylvania campaign can be seen as one of the most successful fulfillments of AFSCME's historical quest to forge a real professional government service — a quest that traced its roots all the way back to Arnold Zander's original efforts in Wisconsin in 1932.

During the struggle to reinstate the transportation department employees, McEntee's campaign gained even more momentum, when AFSCME gained exclusive bargaining representation in a run-off election against PennEl. Eight months later saw the signing of the first statewide unit contract, covering approximately 17,500 members, leading to further organizing successes. McEntee recalls, "We just had meeting after meeting after meeting. I would have to go hoarse four times a week. I remember standing on a flatbed truck in Lebanon County; standing on a Coke box in Fulton

County; in a garage in Cumberland County. I remember trying to debate the laborers and operating engineers and taking an empty chair with me because they wouldn't show up to debate us in front of the workers."

Victories followed in every other state employee category across Pennsylvania. In three and one-half years, AFSCME secured the bargaining rights for 75,000 people. Even as his organizing drives continued, McEntee, in late June 1971, entered into negotiations with the Shapp administration. The result: an agreement that established a 5-percent wage boost, group life insurance, health coverage and language that forever ended the patronage system. During negotiations, AFSCME won its second election, as 21,000 human services workers overwhelmingly approved membership. During next two years, 76,000 state employees in inspection services, investigation and safety units, corrections and psychiatric aides, clerical, administrative and technical services joined the union now increasingly known simply as "Big Green."

9

Building on Success

The union's unprecedented successes in Pennsylvania in early 1971 were one of many historic developments in the union during this period. Through the efforts of organizer Al Bilik, AFSCME expanded with the mergers of the 19,200-member Hawaii Government Employees Association and the 8,400-member United Public Workers of Hawaii. In the first four months of that year alone, AFSCME gained 56,600 new members.

McEntee's successful challenge to Pennsylvania's old, Draconian labor laws for public employees also opened up new possibilities for other sections of the state's public sector workforce. Long overlooked in wage increases and without much say in their everyday work conditions, Philadelphia's upper level professional and technical workers remained outside labor's protections, barred from formal collective bargaining representation. With the shifts in state law after 1970, the men and women in these ranks formed a new section of AFSCME, establishing the city's white-collar District Council 47. Over the next few years, this group of social workers and other professional workers would change the Philadelphia labor movement, backing progressive social programs and building effective coalitions in the communities. Act 195 also made it possible for hospital workers to run organizing campaigns with the protections of the law, spurring the growth of District Council 1199C, which affiliated with AFSCME in 1989.

As the various sections of commonwealth workers came into AFSCME, the Pennsylvania Organizing Committee was formalized as Council 13. Made up of eight district councils from regions across the state, 13 held its founding convention in February 1973. McEntee was unanimously elected executive director. He promised continued growth and progress over the coming years. In July, he and Governor Shapp signed the union's first master agreement, which provided for a 6.5-percent wage increase in each of the two years of the contract.

Jerry McEntee's bold organizing drive had established him as one of the most promising young labor leaders in the United States. In the years following 1973, AFSCME organizing teams often traveled to Harrisburg to consult with McEntee on similar organizing drives in Massachusetts, Washington, New Jersey and Ohio. "Once we got in the saddle in Pennsylvania, AFSCME would send folks in to meet with us, so we could go over our organizing model and why it had worked," McEntee recalls. "Nobody called it 'the model,' but many people wanted to know what we had done and how we had pulled it off."

McEntee established himself as a leader in other ways. He established a Council 13 Education Department that oversaw a regular Leadership Training Program for new officers coordinated at Pennsylvania State University. Reminiscent of the La Salle College labor education programs that instructed Bill McEntee back in the early 1940s, the new initiative introduced AFSCME activists to important skill sets such as parliamentary and grievance procedures, public speaking, labor law and collective bargaining.

The Pennsylvania campaign demonstrated AFSCME's ability to merge politics with organizing. To maximize the union's political clout in 1972, Wurf established the Public Employees Organized for Political and Legislative Equality (PEOPLE), a political action committee that sought to gain legislative support for public workers. In addition, to strengthening an agenda for public employees nationwide, Wurf orchestrated political clout by joining with the National Education Association and the International Association of Firefighters to form the 3-million-member Coalition of American Public Employees.

Commenting on AFSCME's surge after the Zander years, Wurf attributed it to this successful blending of workplace and legislative activism: "Before we were afraid to politicize the union, and we got nowhere, so now we are political as hell." Usually overlooked by the industrial unions that dominated the AFL-CIO councils, the federation established the

Public Employees Department to address the needs of this growing segment of the national labor movement.

In the 1970s, public workers — led by AFSCME — continued to win organizing and collective bargaining victories. In addition, the union fought for better health services for children and the elderly, pensions that allowed for retirement options for older workers, and increased opportunities for minorities, women and youth.

In the early '70s, these goals were becoming part of the mainstream of the nation's politics. One indicator of this new era was support for changes in the nation's public sector labor-relations laws. Coming out of debates over ways on how to bring more order to the contentious government labor relations of the 1960s, AFSCME leaders, championed by a range of other trade unions, labor scholars, legal experts and politicians, supported federal legislation that would grant full collective-bargaining rights for public employees.

Said Wurf at the time, "We decided that it made much more sense to seek relief through a federal law than to dribble out our lives trying to convince 50 state legislatures, 5,000 city councils, and 10,000 school boards and who knows how many other public bodies to devise an impartial mechanism at the lower level." Reflecting the efforts of community allies, religious groups and civil rights organizations around the country, public opinion was strongly in favor of the measure, and many considered its adoption inevitable.

Another key to AFSCME's momentum in the '70s was its ability to connect its goals as a labor organization to those of other emerging social movements. Foremost among these was the growing demand among women for full equality in American society. Energized by the feminist struggles a decade earlier, working-class women stepped up their calls for a transformation of the nation's gender norms. Women activists took the lead in asserting such demands within the AFL-CIO. In 1974, the Coalition of Labor Union Women (CLUW), a national advocacy group of women urged unions to give more attention to the issues of working class women. Many women in AFSCME, including Judith Heh and Wanda Weaver, took a lead in this emerging movement.

McEntee notes the importance of women's activism during these years: "In the beginning, the Pennsylvania state employees were mostly men — because the first unit was trades and labor, which in those days was almost one hundred percent made up of men. But the second big bargaining unit to join AFSCME was institutional workers, who were mostly working in hospitals as aides, LPNs and practical nurses, who were mostly women. Add to that the clerical unit of 21,000, overwhelmingly women."

The sheer density of women within Pennsylvania's AFSCME membership transformed the type of unionism that developed in these years, and it was matched by similar conditions in AFSCME across the United States. "Having so many women in Council 13 definitely shaped the kinds of issues we focused on," McEntee says. "Issues like how to address and end sexual harassment, how to gain maternity leave and medical leave in our contracts. All of this was really new. It did change what AFSCME could be, even if it was a subtle change."

By the end of 1973, McEntee and Council 13 established one of the union's first and largest women's committees. In its initial meetings, the committee gave priority to the development of leadership skills among women leaders, a goal that laid the groundwork for annual women's conferences that continue to this day. Also, women leaders like Heh and Weaver called for the exploration of ways that creation of childcare facilities could become a priority in contract negotiations. As a result of these AFSCME priorities, day care centers for Pennsylvania state workers became a reality in the 1980s.

Of vital importance to the cause of women's equality in the nation's workplaces was the call for pay equity. A major priority of CLUW, this issue placed the gender wage disparity at the center of labor discussions by the mid-1970s. AFSCME helped found the National Coalition on Pay Equity, which continues to research and lobby for change through federal legislation and policy initiatives.

At the 1972 AFSCME Convention, an Interim Committee on Sex Discrimination was formed to study conditions women faced in the public sector workplace. In an important development on this front, AFSCME's Washington state Local 793 (Council 28) pressured Governor Daniel Evans (R) to conduct a wage survey. The results made plain the gender divisions in the state workplace: women were paid 15 to 35 percent less than men. Helen Castrilli, a secretary in a Washington state hospital, remembered, "I used to look out my window, and I'd see a male gardener. He cut the lawn, raked the lawn, did a little trimming under supervision, and he was paid more — several hundred dollars more a month

— than the rest of the women at the hospital [Western State Hospital] who were involved in the 'clerical field.'"

Even after the wage survey, Washington state politicians did nothing to level the field. With women continuing to demand action, AFSCME took the issue up when AFSCME Council 28's executive director asked Castrilli to be a plaintiff in a federal case against the state on the comparable-worth issue. In December 1985, Judge Jack Tanner ruled in favor of AFSCME, with a $101-million pay award for 35,000 women state employees. The back pay made a major change for women like Helen Castrilli. After 30 years of service, she retired. "My retirement was based on my two highest years of state employment. Those two highest years were impacted by the comparable worth increase, and that's forever." The victory enabled Castrilli to send her daughter to the University of Washington.

Emerging from the educational efforts of these years, AFSCME continued to push for fundamental changes in the ways women were treated in jurisdictions from Maine to California. In 1981, San Jose, Local 101 went on strike to get local government officials to finally address the pocketbook disparities.

"To go out on strike over this issue had never been done before," McEntee notes, "and the fact that these women had the guts to do that says so much about their fighting spirit and their vision for what this country can be like — one where one's daughter can have as much chance for success as one's son." Through this job action — which gained national media attention and again highlighted the power of women in Big

Green — Local 101 secured guarantees of higher pay for classifications that traditionally had high numbers of women.

McEntee sought to develop a union that encouraged maximum participation by its members. Through social gatherings and regular conferences, the large statewide organization showed a remarkable sense of unity. Leading into the next round of statewide negotiations in spring and summer 1975, McEntee expected to make further improvements to the contract. However, negotiations stalled when Governor Shapp announced that he would not accept AFSCME's wage demands.

Council 13's democracy then played a part. Remembering the events of this time, McEntee states: "We were in negotiations for a relatively long period of time. Wurf was president — and my relationship with him was up and down. But now I wasn't under Wurf, I was the elected director of Council 13. We had built the union so that people were dramatically and numerically involved. We had what we called Unity Committees — 600 people, and they put the demands together. In addition, we had a negotiation committee of over 200 people. We could tell the damned state anything we wanted, yell at them. I don't think anyone had ever done that before."

In the months leading up to the contract deadline, McEntee mobilized Council 13's members to come to the state Capitol, bringing 25,000 unionists wearing green T-shirts and waving green banners. "They're testing us," McEntee said to the crowds gathered near the Capitol. "They're testing our union. They're testing us to see what we're made of, to see if we have a union," In his ability to ring Harrisburg's state government complexes with so many members — effectively shutting down the city for the day — McEntee demonstrated Council 13's power. In addition, he orchestrated dramatic displays for the media, holding mock funerals for dead government workers, carrying wooden caskets up the stairs of the state legislature. Other acts of civil disobedience — from boisterous sit-ins outside the governor's office to protests on the lawns of lawmakers opposed to AFSCME's demands — brought pressure on state managers.

With such moves impacting the 1975 settlement, McEntee believed that the ultimate use of force — an official strike action — could be averted. "We were finally on our way to settling. Then our people started saying that a 6-percent wage increase wasn't enough. We called another meeting outside Harrisburg on a Sunday afternoon. We had big chicken dinners because we figured we'd stay a while, vote the contact up or down. One of the members gets up. I still remember his name — Ed Harry. He says, 'You know Jerry, we all went over this contract, and it's not worth it. So I recommend we go on strike, starting tomorrow morning.'"

I said, "Are you sure about that, Ed?"

The whole room yelled back the approval of what their spokesman had just said. "We put it to a vote, and it carried unanimously," McEntee says. "As a matter of fact, we ended up with all that chicken."

McEntee found himself leading a massive strike that he had not expected just a few days before. The next day, the whole state was closed down — 76,000 commonwealth employees, walking picket lines that clogged the streets of the state capital and gained attention in every newspaper in the nation. The major Philadelphia papers — the *Inquirer* and the *Bulletin* — and the *Pittsburgh Press* ran big editorials on the walkout. A political cartoon showed the states of New Jersey and Ohio with a sign in the middle saying "Pennsylvania Closed."

The solidarity on picket lines and rallies during that strike has long been remembered by the union's subsequent generations. Wanda Weaver, who already was known as a founder of the union in Harrisburg, secured an even more legendary status following her militant actions in the strike. In a showdown between picketers and about twenty Pennsylvania state troopers, Weaver refused to leave the Capitol steps when ordered to do so. Two troopers picked her up forcibly by her shoulders and hair, dragging her down dozens of concrete steps. When she was finally handcuffed on the sidewalk, she was so bruised that she couldn't stand.

The strike continued over the next few days. There was tension, McEntee says, between the council and AFSCME headquarters: "Wurf tried to kill us, tried to stab us in the back. He wanted to go into negotiations by himself. It got pretty bad. We had the state closed for three days, there were 35 injunctions against us and I was in hiding. We had to eventually settle — on the same terms that we had proposed before. Wurf was on our head, and it was tough being hit with injunctions. It was tough, too, getting our people to buy the settlement," The strike had lasted three days and produced an agreement for an 11-percent wage increase spread over three years.

The three-day walkout and its extensive coverage in the national media had made McEntee a nationally known figure. He had been tested in the largest public-employee strike in U.S. history, and had proved able to lead his members while moving toward a settlement with state managers. The strike had other implications for AFSCME's position in Pennsylvania and across the country. For one thing, as Ed Keller puts it about Council 13, "the strike made us a union." With AFSCME again having proved itself a fighting organization, capable of gaining better standards of living for its members, membership increased in the months and years following.

The summer of 1975 marked, in some ways, the high tide of public sector labor militancy of this era. Besides AFSCME's strike in the Keystone State, sanitation workers in New York City and firefighters in Seattle had mounted picket lines, making front page news across the nation. All of these struggles proved successful for the unions.

On the other hand, their actions gave rise to new political opposition across the country, in part driven by the nation's financial problems and by a rising right-wing movement. The growing fiscal crisis of the 1970s stymied local government growth and limited federal investment in government services at all levels. Increasing numbers of Americans focused on anti-tax platforms that would cut public services. A fierce anti-unionism — focused on public workers — stood at the core of the new right-wing programs, which were supported by such groups as the Public Service Research Council. With the backing of affluent sponsors, Republican activists sought to limit and destroy the very right of public workers to join unions. By the end of 1976, the push toward a Wagner Act for Public Employees, which many observers had believed inevitable just a few years before, had run aground.

This period of uncertainty for America's public workers was exacerbated by the failure of the presidency of Jimmy Carter. Facing economic setbacks all through his years in office, and beset with disastrous foreign policy developments, including the Iranian Hostage Crisis, Carter's 1980 re-election campaign had only cool support from the American labor movement. (Wurf was one of a handful of national labor leaders who had supported Carter in 1976, and was sorely disappointed.) Carter, a moderate Democrat from Georgia, had few labor connections, and he failed to comprehend the needs of working Americans. Measures for full employment and the substantial reform of labor legislation fell short, lacking strong leadership from the Oval Office.

By 1980, liberal Democrats and most sections of organized labor had fallen out with the President, many refusing to endorse him. Disgusted with Carter's performance, Wurf declared that labor must look for a better candidate. They found him: Senator Edward M. Kennedy of Massachusetts.

Kennedy and McEntee were to become lifelong friends and important allies. At their initial meeting, McEntee presented the senator with a political button from John F. Kennedy's 1960 Presidential run, a memento that Teddy appreciated. When he attended the Council 13 convention in 1980, Kennedy entered the hall to cheering delegates. McEntee recalls, "He walked up to the stage to where my father was and shook his hand first. I don't quite know how he knew it was my father, but he did it because he was a smart politician. Everybody loved that."

That summer, McEntee was a delegate for Kennedy at the Democratic convention — a fact he always expresses with pride. Like many labor leaders that year, McEntee believed that the party needed to return to its liberal principals and place working Americans at the heart of national policy. Faced with division within the party's base, Carter stood little chance of re-election, and in November, Ronald Reagan defeated him in one of the most consequential elections of the late 20th century. As was soon evident in the opening months of his first term, Ronald Reagan championed a radical set of principals that would have a heavy negative impact on American labor for years to come.

In late 1981, Ted Kennedy was the first prominent politician to call and congratulate McEntee on his election as AFSCME president, which meant a lot to the labor leader. "He was also the first to call me when my father died in 1983," McEntee remembers. "I don't know how he found that out, but he did. Of course, he had had a tough life, with all of the siblings who died, as well as his own father. We had a lot of things in common. He was just a wonderful human being, a real liberal, a real progressive. We would fight for the same causes, fight like hell."

10

Taking a Big Step Up

By the end of the 1970s, Jerry Wurf's dream of making AFSCME the foremost voice for America's working families was in many ways a reality. With the merger of the 220,000 member New York Civil Service Employees Association (CSEA) into AFSCME in April 1978, AFSCME reached the 1-million-member mark and became a bigger powerhouse on the American political stage. Yet the union also faced an uncertain era, beset with many paradoxes. While AFSCME was gaining members, the majority of powerful industrial unions across the nation were going into decline, as industrial manufacturing centers closed or relocated overseas.

And at AFSCME International, in the early months of 1980, a growing climate of chaos ensued, as Wurf's sometimes-abrupt personal style led to a flurry of resignations or dismissals. Wurf's leadership was also less effective because his rapidly declining health kept him away from the International's headquarters for days at a time.

As AFSCME's top leaders across the country realized that Wurf's health was in serious decline, many began to contemplate who his replacement might be. Even before the 1980 AFSCME Convention, some in the union, especially DC 37 President Victor Gotbaum, quietly urged McEntee to challenge Wurf for the office. McEntee refused, believing that Wurf maintained a strong power base in all regions of the union; and McEntee supported him for re-election at the Convention. Reflecting on his relationship with Wurf, McEntee says, "It was like blood and sand, or oil and fire. It was very, very good some times and very, very bad other times."

In December 1981, Jerry Wurf passed away. McEntee went to Washington, D.C., for the funeral service and declared his candidacy for the presidency. Gotbaum and Secretary-Treasurer William Lucy also ran. The day after the funeral, AFSCME's International Executive Board (IEB) elected McEntee as the union's third International president. Delegates at every AFSCME biennial Convention since then have re-elected him to the office, until his retirement at the 2012 Los Angeles Convention.

McEntee was well aware of the stressful climate that existed at the union headquarters by the end of Wurf's reign. In the year before his death, there had been numerous firings. In one sense, McEntee was running against the revolving door personnel practices of Wurf, and had no intention of continuing them.

Even with this policy made clear, many International staff were concerned about their job security with the shift in power in late 1981. "The afternoon after Jerry won the election, the story goes that AFSCME's Public Affairs Director Phil Sparks went up to Jerry's hotel room at the Hilton and said *The New York Times* wanted to talk to him, and if he wanted, he'd get them on the phone," recounts McEntee aide Paul Booth. "Jerry said sure, and Phil, reflecting his nervousness about his job security, picks up Jerry's hairdryer and hands it to him."

McEntee had a clear vision for AFSCME. Determined to build the most talented political and organizing operation in the American labor movement, he placed an emphasis on staff development and internal recruitment from among the union's officers and rank and file. He wanted to give more power to the IEB and more to the members.

Even with Wurf's emphasis on building national power, the union's Political Department was still somewhat "primitive" when the 1980s began. Wurf had laid the groundwork for an organization with high-caliber professional operations, and McEntee built on that in the coming decade, with AFSCME's political operations becoming even larger and more advanced than the AFL-CIO's.

McEntee also brought a singular leadership style to his presidency. Lee Saunders noted the way he "pushes staff to think outside the box, to propose things that we've not always done in the past. He's always made it clear to staff that they would not be hurt or harmed if they had an idea that we'd never thought of before."

"He's got an incredible sense of humor," Saunders also notes. "He would walk into important meeting with AFSCME nurses, and he'd be wearing a medical coat and a stethoscope. Or he walks into a serious meeting with a mask on just to break the ice, to make people feel more comfortable. Jerry would make the place fun. We know we are doing important work and we know we have an impact on a lot of lives across the country, but he would make it fun and you'd enjoy doing it."

McEntee realized the political difficulties he faced. With Ronald Reagan in the White House, the American labor movement did not have a friend at the top. In one of the important decisions of his first year in office, Reagan summarily fired almost 12,000 members of the striking Professional Air Traffic Controllers Organization, a union that, ironically, had endorsed the President just a year before. Under Reagan, organized labor was promised no place at the table of power. McEntee understood this before his first month in office was over.

Recalling his own first year as president, McEntee says, "I came into the office around the holiday season, and I had a Christmas card from Ronald Reagan. The problem was that it was addressed to Jerry Wurf. The next year, I got the same thing, a card addressed to Wurf. That's how relevant we were."

AFSCME members faced real challenges during the Reagan era. Among the political realities — and problems — was a stream of right-wing political rhetoric, with Reagan himself one of its main purveyors. In his 1981 inaugural address, for example, Reagan declared that "Government is not the solution to our problems, government is the problem." Around the country, AFSCME leaders sought to shape a new rhetoric of their own, one which reinforced the importance and civic need for dedicated public service.

Reagan's proposed cuts in social programs threatened the jobs of AFSCME members across the country. With federal cutbacks, states faced increased financial pressures — especially on hospitals, prisons and child care facilities. In metropolitan centers, the government-service cutbacks led to the closing of state mental-care facilities and a subsequent spike in urban homelessness.

McEntee faced this situation head on, determined to build solidarity among AFSCME's members, across the entire labor movement and with existing and potential community allies. He helped AFSCME position itself to influence federal policy to address the challenges of the Reagan era. He forged new alliances that brought the union wider influence on Capitol Hill. One of his key allies through these difficult years was Ted Kennedy, whose friendship with McEntee, which began in the 1980 campaign, was to prove valuable until the senator's death decades later.

With McEntee's support, the union also took the lead in protecting the rights of public workers from discrimination on the job. For example, in 1982, AFSCME became one of the first unions to support a gay protection clause on its national list of priorities. The push for this development came from Tom Stabnicki and Barry Friedman, activists in AFSCME's Local 2081, which represents social workers in the Illinois Department of Children and Family Services. AFSCME's resolution became a model for others across the nation; the AFL-CIO soon issued its own resolutions against workplace discrimination on the basis of sexual orientation and in favor of increased funding for AIDS research.

"We used union power to create collective bargaining agreements to protect LGBT public employees," McEntee noted years later. "Those victories helped pave the way for non-discrimination policies in the private sector." He pushed for the inclusion of national LGBT groups such as the Human Rights Campaign to be given membership in the Leadership Conference on Civil and Human Rights. He backed the creation of Pride at Work and encouraged the creation of AFSCME Pride, union organizations committed to LGBT equality. His support for LGBT rights continued throughout his years as AFSCME president, including newspaper ads the union took out in opposition to the military's Don't Ask, Don't Tell policy; AFSCME was the only national union to take such a step.

McEntee co-founded the Economic Policy Institute, a leading voice and research organization for working Americans on the economy. When Jeff Faux, founder of EPI, first came to Washington, McEntee organized fund raising events on its behalf, and introduced Faux to other influential labor leaders and political activists around the country. Faux calls McEntee "the rare labor leader who understands the power of ideas."

McEntee also sought to energize AFSCME retirees, convinced that they could become a powerful partner in the battles the union would face throughout his years as president. The growth in this area was spectacular. What began as six chapters of 13,000 retirees in 1980 grew to 100,000 members when New York's CSEA Retiree Division affiliated in the mid-1980s. CSEA's affiliation alone brought in 38,000 retiree members, and the AFSCME Retiree Program became an official department of the International union. By 2012, AFSCME Retirees had grown to more than 250,000 dues-paying retiree members in 41 retiree chapters and 260 local groups. It is the largest public-sector retiree organization in the U.S. and the fastest growing retiree organization in the labor movement.

Although AFSCME had contended with the privatization of public services in its jurisdictions throughout its history, the 1980s placed this issue at the center of many unions around the nation. Indeed, by 1987, the average American city contracted out 27 percent of its municipal services, a number that some commentators believed would increase even further in the decade to come. McEntee authorized an aggressive response to such proposals, devising union strategies against contracting out in regional leadership seminars and highlighting successful stories of union victories in AFSCME's national publication, *Public Employee.*

AFSCME's researchers warned that privatization would result in higher costs and, more important, a loss of accountability to the taxpayer. Where elected officials were accountable to citizens, a third party was not. AFSCME asserted that public service was an honorable calling. With emphasis on the bottom line, contractors would cut corners to maximize profit. Work provided by private contractors only saved money for cities because it would ultimately be based on an informal labor pool that provided workers with few or no benefits and lower wages — both of which negatively impacted the community.

11

Expanding AFSCME

AFSCME took a more determined approach — workplace by workplace — in addressing the threat of service cuts. Even in the face of overall union decline and in the face of aggressively anti-union political opponents, AFSCME continued to expand, building powerful organizations among correctional officers, nurses, child care workers, social workers and state employees in campaigns in Illinois, Nebraska and Ohio.

In one of the more memorable unionization campaigns of the late 1980s, AFSCME helped gain a contract for 3,500 members of the Harvard Union of Clerical and Technical Workers. Founded in 1986 as an independent organization of non-teaching staff, mostly office and laboratory employees, the HUCTW was a model of the new kind of trade unionism that brought together elements of the women's rights movement and community activism. Boosted by a heightened workplace social consciousness that came from the feminist movement, Harvard's employees succeeded in gaining tangible benefits and, of equal importance, a voice on the job.

McEntee's original organizing vision in Pennsylvania remained an important inspiration for similar mass organizing drives throughout his presidency. AFSCME succeeded in gaining collective bargaining rights for Indiana state employees, and the union launched a major recruitment drive in 1990. The campaign would prove to be a significant turning point for both the national union and the broader labor movement.

Recalling that period, McEntee observes: "We had a small union in Indiana, mostly comprised of a handful of state employees and some counties and cities and things like that. It wasn't a very strong union, but it was the only union in town." Governor Evan Bayh agreed to support the right to bargain collectively, and AFSCME began to organize. As had happened in previous jurisdictions, the labor movement was divided, with different unions jockeying in the election campaign for the loyalties of potential members. In Indiana, the UAW collaborated with the AFT to form a united coalition to support state employees.

That would prove a particularly difficult contest, and one with broad implications for how unions operated in the years to come. McEntee recalls it as "a very ugly campaign." McEntee recalls: "The teachers had some strength, in the cities, the counties and in various school districts. The UAW in Indiana was very, very strong, because they had auto plants and stuff like that. They were better equipped than we were, because they get their people in the plants off to help with the organizing. You'd go up to a hospital, there would be like one hundred UAW people there, and we'd have like five."

The friction between the competing unions broke into the open, with organizers and their supporters engaging in fistfights. Even under such conditions, and outnumbered, McEntee and other AFSCME leaders believed they would win. Yet the union's polls proved inaccurate: AFSCME lost in one of their strongest sections, Indiana's Correctional Officers, and the combined front of autoworkers and teachers captured most of the bargaining units. AFSCME's organizers, McEntee remembers, "were afraid to call with the results."

From this confrontational campaign, a new spirit of cooperation emerged between AFSCME, the UAW and other unions. To McEntee, that only made sense: "You ought to get together and not kill one another, because both unions have money, both know how to organize, so we realized we ought to do the very best we could to see if we can work together."

By the mid-1990s, that philosophy had taken hold, thanks to a McEntee-spearheaded reform movement that would transform the operation of the national labor movement, streamlining organizing campaigns to maximize cooperation between unions. The AFL-CIO, for example, adopted Article XXI and created a mediation and arbitration process to resolve competing organizing claims by national unions. The goal was to end wasteful competition in an era when a substantial majority of workers remain unorganized, and it has largely been achieved.

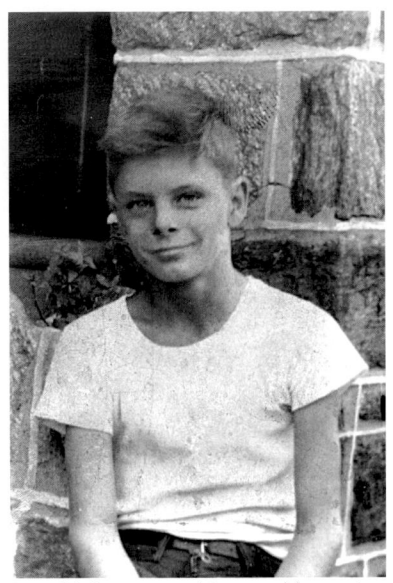

Jerry McEntee as a 10-year old growing up in Philadelphia.

McEntee's father, William, led a 1939 strike by Philadelphia sanitation workers that resulted in AFSCME's first collectively bargained contract in a major city.

From left, Bernard "Buck" Martin, Edward J. Keller, McEntee and Pasquale "Pat" Salvatore – the four original members of AFSCME's Pennsylvania Organizing Committee – in February 1970, moments after becoming the first public employees union to be voluntarily recognized by an employer (City of Lancaster).

AFSCME Council 13 Executive Director McEntee watches as Pennsylvania Governor Milton Shapp signs a the 1972 contract with clerical workers with Bob Settle, AFSCME area coordinator, left, and longtime activist Wanda Weaver, behind Shapp, looking on.

AFSCME President Jerry Wurf, right, greets McEntee at the 1974 International Convention in Honolulu, Hawaii.

McEntee acknowledged a standing ovation from the members at the 1982 AFSCME International Convention in Atlantic City, N.J., his first as president. He had been elected the previous year by the International Executive Board after the death of Jerry Wurf, and served out Wurf's remaining term until 1984 when he was elected by the membership.

In November of 1984, McEntee was arrested outside the South African embassy in Washington, DC, as part of Free South Africa Movement anti-apartheid protests.

McEntee spoke at a Coalition of Labor Union Women Conference (CLUW) in 1984 as Lane Kirkland, president of the AFL-CIO, and Joyce Miller, president of CLUW, looked on.

Nobel Peace Laureate Nelson Mandela received a tumultuous ovation when he appeared at the 1990 AFSCME International Convention in Miami, just months after his release from 27 years in prison.

President Bill Clinton listens intently to McEntee behind stage at the 2000 Democratic National Convention in Los Angeles.

McEntee at the podium of the 2000 Democratic National Convention in Los Angeles when Vice President Al Gore was nominated for president.

McEntee knocking on doors in Philadelphia during the 2000 presidential campaign for Al Gore.

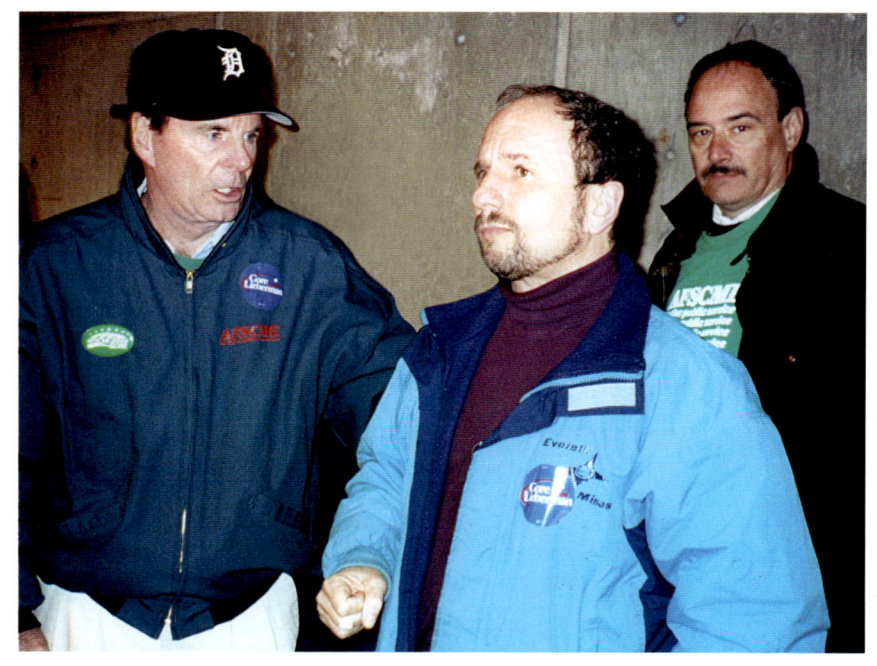

McEntee campaigning with U.S. Sen. Paul Wellstone in 2000. Larry Scanlon, at right, is director of the AFSCME Political Action department.

Joining McEntee for the 2000 anniversary march commemorating the 1968 Memphis Sanitation Workers strike were, from left, Willie "Joe" Alexander, AFSCME Local 1733 president; Tajuan Stout Mitchell, Memphis City Councilwoman; Myron Lowrey, Memphis City Councilman; Rickey Peete, Memphis City Councilman; and Adjua Naantaanbuu, founder of the first Southern Christian Leadership Conference (SCLC) Chapter, who picked up Dr. King at the airport when he arrived in Memphis to support the sanitation workers.

McEntee (in green hat and jacket) marched in Tallahassee with other prominent activists in the Coalition of Conscience event to demand a fair count of Florida's votes in the 2000 Gore-Bush presidential race.

President McEntee and Assistant to the President Lee Saunders toured Ground Zero shortly after the 9/11 attacks in 2001.

McEntee joined Las Vegas culinary workers on a picket line during the 2002 AFSCME International Convention in Las Vegas.

McEntee reacts to a question from a member during the 2004 International Convention in Anaheim, Calif.

McEntee led the fight in 2005 to protect Social Security from President George W. Bush's plan to privatize it. Here he mobilizes a crowd at a U.S. Capitol rally.

McEntee enjoys a laugh at the 2005 Western Region Women's Conference in San Jose, Calif.

McEntee leads a joint union rally for Human Rights/Workers Rights in Washington, DC, in 2005.

McEntee receives a welcoming lei at an AFSCME Retirees meeting during the 2006 International Convention in Chicago. Steve Regenstreif (left) director of the AFSCME Retirees department, and Jerry LaPoint, chair of the Retirees, had already received their welcoming leis.

President McEntee surveyed the hall during rehearsals for the 2006 AFSCME International Convention in Chicago. McEntee's Executive Assistant Paul Booth is at right.

John Sweeney, president of the AFL-CIO, was present in 2007 when McEntee celebrated his 25 years as president of AFSCME.

Senator Barack Obama visited President McEntee in his office during the presidential campaign of 2008.

Children joined McEntee on stage during a rally by Connecticut Council 4 in 2008 that protested privatization by Aramark.

McEntee joined the PEOPLE Fun Run at the AFSCME International Convention in 2008 in San Francisco.

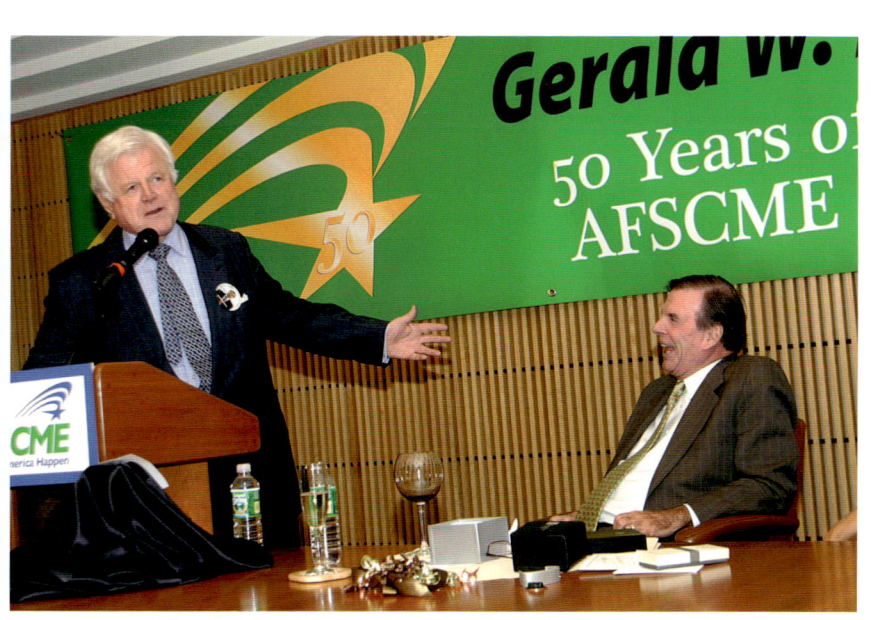

Senator Edward "Ted" Kennedy congratulated McEntee for his 50 years of service to the union at an event held at AFSCME headquarters in 2009.

McEntee joined AFSCME's Highway to Health Care staff who traveled the country for months in 2009 in a specially outfitted bus to promote health care reform.

McEntee spoke to 150,000 people — including members of Servidores Públicos Unidos de Puerto Rico, Concilio 95 AFSCME — who turned out on a hot day in 2009 for a one-day general strike protesting the radical Law 7 that attacked public service employees.

McEntee spoke to tens of thousands of people on a cold February day in 2011 at the Wisconsin State Capitol in Madison after Governor Scott Walker proposed a law — that the Legislature eventually passed — stripping union workers of their collective bargaining rights.

McEntee spoke to AFSCME's young activists and leaders at the Next Wave Conference in Atlanta in 2011.

McEntee with Speaker of the House Nancy Pelosi (above), and with his wife Barbara (right) at the December 7, 2011, Working America event, which honored McEntee for his 55 years with AFSCME.

McEntee horseback riding in Wyoming in 1998.

12

Target: National Political Influence

With the collapse of the Soviet bloc in Eastern Europe through the summer of 1989, and the fall of the Berlin Wall that November, the Cold War had come to an unexpectedly swift end. In South Africa, years of political oppression under the racist apartheid regime cracked, and Nelson Mandela was released from prison in 1990, leading to South Africa's first popular elections a few years later. Long a supporter of the anti-apartheid struggle, McEntee had been arrested, along with Secretary-Treasurer Lucy and other labor leaders at the South African embassy. In 1990, on his first trip to the United States, Mandela addressed the 1990 AFSCME Convention and paid tribute to the efforts of the American labor movement to end apartheid.

With the end of the Cold War, McEntee believed that a new era of possibilities awaited AFSCME. Cuts in national military budgets could ultimately strengthen federal commitments to improved social services at home, creating more opportunities for AFSCME members across the country.

McEntee believed that the Democratic Party had a strong chance at retaking the White House from President George H.W. Bush in 1992. Bush's economic policies had led to economic decline, as hundreds of thousands of Americans lost their jobs, including public employees throughout the country.

McEntee and the labor movement were committed to putting together a winning ticket that championed the cause of working families for the 1990s. In the first stages of this effort, McEntee looked to place at the helm of the Democratic Party someone who, going into the election year, would strongly advance a pro-worker agenda. McEntee, along with then-Rep. Bill Richardson (D-NM) and others, pushed successfully for Ron Brown to become party chairman in 1991.

McEntee remembers: "I knew Ron Brown well, we were in politics together, we were very tight. He was gutsy, he was progressive, he understood working people. He was also sharp — he could be out in the public scene, but he could work behind the scenes as well."

With this important part in place, McEntee and AFSCME's leadership continued to look for the right candidate for 1992. The previous November, he invited the Democratic candidates in the field — Tom Harkin, Bob Kerrey, Bill Clinton, Paul Tsongas and Jerry Brown — to interview with AFSCME's executive board. Three showed up: Harkin, Kerrey and Clinton. McEntee knew that board members would have a keen ear for what their members wanted in a presidential candidate. The selection process was wide open.

Senator Kerrey met with McEntee and other AFSCME leaders in Detroit. Kerrey was a popular senator and former Nebraska governor, and he had won the Medal of Honor for his service in Vietnam. He lost the lower part of a leg in combat.

McEntee began the questioning by asking the candidate to explain his plan for health care reform.

Kerrey began to explain the reasons why such reform was necessary.

McEntee then asked, "Enough of that. What's your plan for winning and who are the people who can get you there?"

Kerrey mentioned his campaign team, many of whom came from Nebraska. McEntee was not impressed. He knew that Kerrey's campaign team would not be up to the task of winning a Presidential election. Observing the interview process, one senior AFSCME staffer recalls, "The air went out of the Kerrey balloon. He kept trying to convince us that these guys really knew what they were doing."

One candidate impressed the board more than the others: Arkansas Governor Bill Clinton. Remembering this meeting years later, AFSCME Political Director Larry Scanlon said that Clinton surpassed every other candidate, able to specify the logic behind his health care plan and to outline a convincing program of how he would get it enacted. McEntee concurred: "By the time we had interviewed all of the candidates, there was no question that Bill Clinton was the one ready for prime time. I mean, you asked him questions and bam, bam, bam, he understood the issues. He was walking around the room, doing all of the stuff Clinton does.

"We saw our union becoming a political powerhouse. The culmination of that was when we supported Clinton. AFSCME was the first union to support him, and I felt comfortable enough with our membership to do that. When we pulled the string on that, it made us, made us politically and in a lot of other ways."

While AFSCME's endorsement of the future President may seem completely logical from hindsight, the decision was a considerable risk. Going into 1992, few American voters had ever heard of the former Arkansas governor, who was running fifth among six candidates in New Hampshire polls. McEntee's support of Clinton bonded him with the president. Clinton noted, in November 2006, "Jerry McEntee took a huge chance in endorsing me early when I was running for President…. He has the heart of a lion, and I never had a better friend."

In his autobiography, Clinton noted his friendship with McEntee, which began during the Presidential campaign. McEntee, Clinton wrote, was "effective, fiercely loyal and a man who didn't mind a fight."

With strong AFSCME support, Clinton won the Democratic nomination and went on to defeat George H.W. Bush and Ross Perot in a three-way race for the Oval Office. Soon after taking office, Clinton made good on an important election promise that was high on McEntee's list of priorities — the 1993 Family and Medical Leave Act. The act provided job protection for family members who needed to care for one of their own, including newborn babies and children.

Clinton's progressive health care proposal, which had so impressed AFSCME leaders and become the heart of his 1992 campaign, went down to defeat in his second years as president. McEntee played a key role in that legislative struggle, helping to lobby congressional votes and enlisting support among AFSCME members across the nation. In Washington, the union's lobbyists and McEntee met with Senator Daniel Patrick Moynihan, chairman of the finance committee. At one point, the huge book containing the complex bill slipped from Moynihan's grasp and fell to the floor. McEntee leaned toward an aide and said, "This doesn't look good for where this meeting is headed."

The loss of the health care bill had a severe impact on the Democratic electorate. If anything, Republicans moved even further to the right in the days that followed. Also, by the end of 1993, President Clinton had supported a trade agreement antithetical to American labor: the North American Free Trade Agreement. Supporters of NAFTA argued that it would create U.S. jobs, but it made outsourcing to Mexico much more attractive for U.S. companies and cost hundreds of thousands of American manufacturing jobs.

Democrats were in disarray throughout the 1994 off-year election. They lost the House of Representatives for the first time since the 1950s. The President's approval ratings slipped, and his chances for re-election were greatly diminished.

Coming into power was a new kind of conservative Republican, determined to continue the economic policies of Ronald Reagan. Led by Georgia Rep. Newt Gingrich, whose "Contract with America" proposed deep slashes in social funding, the new congressional majority brought a deeply anti-labor legislative program to the fore. In his policy speeches, House Speaker Gingrich promised to overturn traditional social programs, including Medicare. Bolstered by a right-wing media empire that included talk radio host Rush Limbaugh, the political environment of the mid-1990s was toxic.

In the early months of 1995, McEntee and other union leaders got a fuller sense of the radical programs the Gingrich revolution entailed. McEntee positioned AFSCME behind a defense of Medicare and Medicaid. "McEntee led the charge to fight back," Scanlon recounts. "He put a lot of money and prestige on the line. I think that has been a hallmark of his presidency." Paul Booth credits him with "deciding that he would draw a line in the sand against Gingrich." By the end of 1995, the Republican momentum was to a large degree halted.

Explaining this historic moment further, Booth observes, "This is when Bill Clinton, the President of the United States, was trying to convince reporters that he was still relevant. Clinton was in an ice box, frozen out of the equation. The Democratic leadership in Congress was in retreat mode, and AFSCME sounded the bugle that said the retreating is over, we're going to stand and fight. That was an incredibly important moment. Fighting back is in the Jerry McEntee blood stream."

Coming out of the battle to save Medicare, McEntee reassessed the power of the labor movement to affect substantial change. Labor had been losing members since the early 1970s, with the loss of thousands of industrial jobs in key areas such as steel, auto and textiles. Overall, the movement by the beginning of 1995 was in a state of disrepair. Demoralized, and seeming to lack a broad social program, the AFL-CIO's current leadership, centered on President Lane Kirkland, was out of step with political changes taking place accross America, and more important, out of touch with its members.

Indeed, as labor scholars have noted, the leadership of the movement was mostly older white men, whose primary emphasis had traditionally been Cold War foreign policy. The AFL-CIO under Lane Kirkland had become stodgy; in key areas, like political action and member communications, it was ill equipped.

Years earlier, Jerry Wurf had sought to shift the organization toward embracing more progressive social programs, but to little avail. Now the possibilities of transforming the broader labor movement along similar lines had more potential. By 1995, public sector workers were no longer on the fringes of the central councils of the AFL-CIO. Those workers' unions — with AFSCME in the lead — had the numbers and influence to impact how organized labor worked.

13

The Revolt in the AFL-CIO

Other labor leaders besides McEntee were taking a hard look at the direction of the AFL-CIO, and they, too, were open to new directions. More than anyone else, however, McEntee provided a blueprint for change. By mid-1995, he would almost single-handedly shape an opposition slate in the AFL-CIO to address what he saw as the needs of the American worker in a new economy. Such a revamping, McEntee believed, would be the first step in initiating a new political climate. American labor unions had lost over one million members. To maintain a significant position in the 21st century, organizing would need to be stressed to an unprecedented degree.

McEntee recalls a telling exchange he had with AFL-CIO President Lane Kirkland:

McEntee: "All of the unions were getting banged around, and we all needed whatever help, support, aid we could get. I knew that the treasury of the AFL-CIO was large. So I met with the AFL-CIO president in his office. I said, 'Lane, we're all getting killed out there. You've got money in the treasury. You've got to start helping, moving that money around to help people, help the unions.'"

Kirkland: "No, I'm saving that, Jerry. I am saving that for a rainy day."

McEntee: "Have you looked out the damned window? It's pouring."

Kirkland: "No. No, I can't do it. Can't do it."

"I walked out of the meeting." McEntee continues: "It came time for Lane to run again. We're all at the AFL-CIO for his press conference. He walks from the executive council floor down to the first floor and up to the podium. And he announces to all of the reporters — there must have been about one hundred of them — that he is going to run again for re-election as president. He steps down and walks away, and the press starts to pack up their stuff.

"I walked up onto the podium and said, 'Wait a minute, wait a minute, I want to make an announcement. I am Jerry McEntee, president of AFSCME. This election is going to be unlike any other that we've had, because President Kirkland is going to have opposition.'

"They said, 'Jerry, who's that going to be?'

"I said, 'I'm not permitted to say now.' And then I walked away.

"I had nobody, not a person, in my mind, but my announcement caused quite a stir. A few nights later, I am at a dinner somewhere in Washington, and Bob Strauss comes up to me and says, 'What do you think you're doing?' Strauss had been chairman of the Democratic National Committee from 1972 to 1977. He was an experienced Washington insider.

"I said, 'What do I think I'm doing? Who the hell are you to ask me?'

"He said, 'Lane....'

"I said, 'What about Lane? This doesn't have anything to do with you, man.'"

In the days that followed, McEntee focused on unseating Kirkland, appearing in the audience whenever he spoke: "I followed him around the country. I flew to Los Angeles, where he was speaking. He gives his speech and says, 'Does anybody have any questions?'

"I got up and I took him through the ringer. Tough, tough questions. I forget where the next place was, but I was there, same seat, same hand going up. You could see him starting to burn.

"Finally, at a Chicago appearance, Kirkland said things were going to be a little different. He said, 'There's a gentleman in the room who will be glad to hear what I have to say.' Then he read aloud George Meany's final address and said, 'I am adopting that. I am retiring and leaving the AFL-CIO.'

"I clapped, and the people in the hall picked up the applause."

In the wake of Kirkland's announcement, AFL-CIO Secretary-Treasurer Thomas Donahue announced his candidacy. While McEntee liked Donahue personally, he did not favor him to succeed Kirkland. Some three months earlier, McEntee had talked to Donahue about running, and now the secretary-treasurer was asking for his support for the higher office. McEntee declined to give it.

McEntee said, "We've come to the conclusion that we want to change the whole AFL-CIO. We don't like its direction. We don't like a lot of its people. They don't have a passion any more, or they're worn out. We want all of that changed."

Even at this point, however, McEntee didn't have a candidate in mind. The other dissidents — including Teamsters reform President Ron Carey and the UMW's Rich Trumka — called a meeting at a Washington hotel. "Seven of the top leaders were there, and I ran the meeting with a beer bottle. I said, 'Now we're going to pick who's going to be the next president of the AFL-CIO. First of all, I do not want it. I will not take it. I like where I am, so it's got to be someone else.'

"So we go around the table. John Sweeney doesn't want it, Carey doesn't, nobody wants it except for Rich Trumka. I said, 'You're too young, and you're from a small union. Later on, maybe.' We left the meeting without reaching a decision, although I knew who it should be.

"We were driving back to where John Sweeney and I were staying. He's driving, and he's the worst damned driver in the world. I was scared to death at points. I said, 'John, you're going to take it.'

"He said, 'No, I don't want that.'

"I said, 'Yeah, it's over, John. You're going to take it.'"

Weeks later, Sweeney still refused to go for the position, but McEntee continued to press him. McEntee said, "John, there's a press conference scheduled here in AFSCME's building. It's going to start in about fifteen minutes. I'm announcing that you're running for the presidency of the AFL-CIO.'

"He said, 'Why are you doing that?'

"I said, 'Because you are. That's all.' I hung up the phone, and I went out and made the announcement that John was going to run. The reporters there pointed out that I was announcing that John Sweeney was going to run, but he wasn't even here.

"I said, 'That's all right. He'll be here when it's necessary.'"

In boldly proposing a new direction for the labor federation, McEntee had energized labor activists. In October 1995, John Sweeney and his New Voice coalition won 57 percent of the votes. Along with Sweeney, Richard Trumka was elected secretary-treasurer and Linda Chavez-Thompson executive vice-president. In the months that followed, Sweeney sought to revamp organizing programs within the AFL-CIO and begin a substantial overhaul of the labor movement's political program.

Within months, the new AFL-CIO leadership launched Labor '96, putting $35 million into field organizing and radio and television advertisements to educate working people on issues that mattered in that election year. Sweeney also created Union Summer, a program for young people to learn organizing in the nation's streets and communities.

Reflecting on the Sweeney years, McEntee says, "I think they were tough times, but he gave us a stronger federation, a stronger structure as far as central labor bodies and state federations and things like that. The organizing departments were better funded, and he built a political program that had been very small before."

In 1998, the AFL-CIO closed its Public Employee Department, reasoning that the broader labor movement no longer differed from the public sector unions. McEntee began to lay the groundwork for the role he imagined Big Green playing in the politics of the coming decade, raising dues to generate an extra seven million dollars a year for a nationwide organizing campaign. Such policies had an impact: in the first few years of the decade, after doubling spending on organizing, AFSCME organized 250,000 workers.

Years later, Sweeney jokingly criticized *The New York Times* for stating that McEntee had installed him in the presidency of the AFL-CIO. "Installed me? What's this 'install,'" Sweeney asked mockingly, "What the hell am I, a plumbing fixture?" He has always praised McEntee's efforts to revitalize the labor movement, as both a political and an organizing force. As he noted in 2011, "Jerry not only led that historic change at the AFL-CIO, he's led all of the progressive changes in our movement."

14

Expanding the Union's Horizon

As chairman of the AFL-CIO Political Education Committee, McEntee implemented the ambitious program known as Labor '96. Following the restructuring of the AFL-CIO the previous year, Labor '96 was a concerted effort to re-elect President Clinton and take back as many House seats as possible. In an unprecedented effort, the labor movement pooled $35 million to elect supportive candidates.

At the 1996 Democratic convention, AFSCME delegates represented 25 percent of the labor movement. (If the union had been a state, it would have been the sixth largest.) In a speech he delivered from the podium to all the delegates at the Atlanta convention, McEntee declared, "We have a vision of an America where families get all the medical care they need, not only as much as they can afford. We have a vision of an America where the first question you're asked when you go to a hospital is where does it hurt, not where's your insurance. In short, we have a vision of an America where every family can get ahead and no worker is ever left behind."

AFSCME and Labor '96 had a positive impact in November, with the Clinton-Gore ticket re-elected and the Democrats gaining House seats. As election results came in, it was clear that McEntee's vision of a revitalized labor movement had become a reality. In 1996, union households increased their share of the popular vote to 23 percent, up from 14 two years earlier. Sixty-two percent of those households voted for Democratic congressional candidates.

The results were undeniable: labor's activism — and votes — had swayed the election, despite the fact unions had been outspent by big business by a factor of seven to one. In all regions across the country except the South, Democrats gained seats. McEntee addressed this the night of the election: "Two years ago the radical right would have laughed at the notion that organized labor would become their worst nightmare, but tonight they're not laughing anymore."

As it had in the previous decade, AFSCME continued to grow through the 1990s. In Maryland, for example, after Governor Parris Glendenning signed an executive order allowing collective bargaining for state employees, 40,000 state workers joined AFSCME in the largest union election in six years. With this new voice on the job, workers felt they could address conditions without fear of retribution from politically connected management.

Another important inroad for AFSCME came in Puerto Rico. In 1998, after years of lobbying and political efforts,

140,000 central government employees gained collective bargaining rights. Formed in 1995, the Servidores Públicos Unidos de Puerto Rico (SPU/AFSCME) (United Public Employees of Puerto Rico, in English) had fought a difficult battle. Numerous bargaining-rights proposals had been defeated, despite Governor Rosselló's support. In the years after 1998, AFSCME organizers and activists continued to make improvements for the island's thousands of government workers, making SPU/AFSCME one of the most powerful labor organizations on the island and an important part of the AFSCME family.

McEntee believed in linking political power to organizing campaigns. On his ability to make this happen, his closest advisors speak uniformly. "He understands the nexus of political power and how to use it," Larry Scanlon says. "I've been in the room with him when he's had one of these one on one's with governors, for what they did or didn't do. It was eye opening, jaw dropping, how he spoke to these governors."

AFSCME's California organizing campaigns of the 1990s clearly illustrate this point. In his bid for the California governor's office, AFSCME had placed a lot of resources behind Democrat Gray Davis. In early meetings with Davis, the union's leaders made clear that they wanted to gain agency shop for higher education employees. Important legislators in Sacramento were backing an agency shop bill, and it needed the governor's support, which AFSCME expected after he was elected. However, at the last minute, Davis sent word to Washington that he would withhold his support for unexpected political reasons.

As Scanlon recalls this telephone exchange between McEntee and the governor:

McEntee: "Gray, we had an understanding. We were going to do this agency shop clause."

Davis: "Well, I've got a problem...."

McEntee: "You got a problem? The hell with you!" McEntee slammed down the phone.

The governor called back in ten minutes: "Jerry, I've reconsidered. I think I can do this, I think I can sign this bill."

From such personal pressure, backed by the union's power, AFSCME secured agency shop in California. The state had long been what one McEntee lieutenant calls "a black hole" for AFSCME. But the union poured in resources, and California is now one of the top membership regions. Paul Booth also provides insight into the nature of McEntee's skills. "What he derived from oral culture is a lock-box memory. It is not uncommon among good labor leaders, but he has an extremely sharpened retention of who said what and when and in what sequence. That is reinforced with the most rudimentary notes on a piece of paper that he would write on the back of an envelope. His memory of what happened 17 years ago is more trustworthy than most people."

McEntee also has a firm grasp of what is politically possible. In the California drive, AFSCME's success resulted in part from the fact that the union's demands were simple and straightforward. Booth continues, "There were only two things we wanted: Union security for university employees and employer of record for home care workers — we got both. In contrast, SEIU [the Service Employees International Union] had a list of 20 demands. California is now our second-biggest membership state in the union. Jerry's energy made it possible."

Another area of AFSCME organizing strength over the past generation has been among the nation's correctional officers. With more than 100,000 members from this profession, the union established its own section, AFSCME Corrections United. Facing specific difficulties on the job and a shared set of political obstacles, the ACU represents a powerful bloc within the national body. "Politicians want to lock them up and throw away the key, but they forget that the key is hanging on your belt," McEntee said at the 1995 ACU convention.

Working conditions remain a crucial issue for the union in prisons. Stricter sentencing laws, and the resultant spike in the inmate population, should also lead to expansion of facilities. But in many areas of the country, this has not been the case, leading to dangerous overcrowding that threatens prisoners, officers and the public.

In addition, political decisions have too often connected politicians with privateers who look to prisons as profit makers. McEntee describes the situation this way: "When corporations take over prison management, they fire people, they cut staff way down and then hire anybody who walks in off the street and is willing to work for not much more than the minimum, with few if any benefits and less training than you get as a Boy Scout." The ACU addresses these concerns, while coordinating professional training through regional conferences.

McEntee has maintained his commitment to solidarity within the American labor movement. A clear case in point: his active support for one of the most celebrated union victories of this generation, the six-year struggle at the Frontier Hotel and Casino in Las Vegas. In September 1991, 550 Frontier workers, members of Hotel and Restaurant Employees (HERE), went on strike. The walkout followed the purchase of the hotel by owners Margaret Elardi and her sons, who cut wages and benefits, pensions and basic job security. Worker solidarity was strong, with other locals raising union dues to support the strike fund at HERE Local 226. Workers adopted the slogan "One Day Longer."

In 1992, McEntee decided that AFSCME could play an active role in boosting the morale of the striking brothers and sisters in Las Vegas. At the AFSCME Convention, delegates coordinated the largest single rally of the entire six-year Frontier struggle. "There were 4,000 of us, all in green AFSCME shirts," McEntee proudly recalls. "There were only about 10 pickets, and they saw us and they went absolutely wacko — the Green Machine was here."

Real progress in ending the strike was not made until a Kansas City entrepreneur offered to buy the property from the Elardi family. Within an hour of the purchase, a contract was quickly agreed on — bringing the long dispute to a successful end for the workers. Attending a rally the night of the victory were Nevada's governor and U.S. senators, along with the

Reverend Jesse Jackson and Jerry McEntee. He calls the victory "the most significant in American labor since the early CIO days and Walter Reuther."

"I had never seen a strike end that way," McEntee says. "At midnight, the members voted to end it, and all of the strikers went to the Frontier. I was with them, about the third person in there. I remember one guy leaping over the bar — he was the bartender there when they had voted to strike in 1991, and now he was back. He said, 'I'm the bartender here now!' It was a wonderful thing."

AFSCME has also been on the front lines in the battle to regulate excessive speculation by Wall Street insiders. Long before the financial crisis, McEntee warned of the consequences of a failure to adequately regulate financial markets and corporate boards. He and AFSCME pushed for "Say on Pay" policies and other steps to hold corporate officers accountable to shareholders. When increasing deregulation in the Bush years exploded into a global financial crisis, McEntee's call to make Wall Street more open, accountable and responsible helped spur the passage of President Obama's financial-reform legislation.

In December 1999, AFSCME participated in the mass mobilizations protesting the meeting of the World Trade Organization (WTO) in Seattle. Over the course of three days, more than 40,000 activists came together: labor union members, children's advocates, environmentalists and others. At the heart of this movement was a burning desire to expose the socially irresponsible practices of the WTO, whose market-driven platform bypasses existing labor laws that protect workers' safety, wages and benefits, and seeks to eliminate necessary regulations on business. Hundreds of AFSCME members showed up for the rallies, many from surrounding states. At a rally in a large stadium with thousands of protestors — and before a large AFSCME section, McEntee spoke out: "We are here to change the system: the market system, the profit system. Here we stand on the streets of America, and we say to our corporate leaders, 'Shame on you!'"

15

Combating Corruption

In the 1990s, McEntee dealt with a range of other issues that defined his leadership. One of the most difficult cases involved the discovery of corruption in the union's largest chapter, New York City's 125,000 member District Council 37. An AFSCME flagship that had played a pivotal role in the union's history, the council was rocked by discoveries of fiscal mismanagement and illegal actions. Since 1987, Stanley Hill had overseen DC 37, taking over after Victor Gotbaum retired.

In 1998, the council faced disturbing reports of financial mismanagement. Two presidents of local unions had embezzled almost 1 million dollars, and others billed personal living expenses to the union. Still others were charged with stuffing ballot boxes to ensure ratification of an unpopular contract that stipulated a two-year wage freeze. By the end of the investigation, 22 union officials had been sent to prison.

As the allegations against some of DC 37's leaders became public, questions surfaced in the media about the position the International union would take. There were widespread doubts that the union would act, at least not forcefully. Many of the indicted leaders in New York were McEntee supporters. "But he took it [the problem] head on," recalls Lee Saunders, whom McEntee appointed to administer the New York council. "He held an internal review and took the matter to the district attorney. In addition, he decided that DC 37 needed to be taken over by the International. Many didn't think he would do that, either. It was an overwhelming task."

The challenge Saunders faced was unprecedented in the history of the union. In his first year of oversight, he implemented new methods of financial reporting, including a rigorous auditing system, and the appointment of an impartial ethical practices officer. In all future contract ratifications, a third-party neutral would oversee counting of ballots.

In 2002, AFSCME announced an end to the trusteeship. The union had changed and come through stronger. "I think DC 37 is a vibrant and aggressive union once again," Saunders said about the decision. "It's time it returns to the place where it rightfully belonged." During these years, Saunders also took on the conservative proposals of Mayor Rudolph Giuliani, who boasted of wanting to weaken the union at this moment of restructuring. Through this difficult transitional period in New York, Saunders credits the success to the members in the city. "I had the support of members there. It's like a second home to me."

In the aftermath of the crisis in New York, McEntee believed it was necessary to guard against future problems by holding the entire union to the strict standards adopted in DC 37 under Saunders's direction. "When an organization is as large and as public about fighting for the rights of working families as AFSCME, it becomes an easy target," McEntee observed.

He pushed for reforms, adopted at the 2002 Convention, such as a requirement that the International audit the financial records of all councils and locals with 2,000 or more members — which covers 98 percent of the union's membership. AFSCME also conducts vigorous training for financial staff. "Most important," McEntee says, "when our stringent internal accountability process uncovers wrongdoing, we remove violators from office, help prosecute them when appropriate and work to correct any improprieties as quickly as possible."

16

The New Millennium

By 2000, Jerry McEntee could look back on the previous ten years as an era which he had helped to shape, one in which AFSCME realized its potential to be one of the most powerful voices for working Americans in the nation. The Clinton years had been prosperous ones, and McEntee believed that, with continued political success, they could lead to an even greater period of improvement for members and working people everywhere.

Reflecting on the state of the country at the end of his years in the White House, President Clinton noted: "Never before has our nation enjoyed, at once, so much prosperity and social progress with so little internal crisis and so few external threats." In a farewell to Clinton at AFSCME's 2000 Convention in Philadelphia, McEntee presented him with an original copy of the Lincoln-Douglas debates as a testament to his commitment to civil rights and activism. Reflecting the theme of the Convention — The Future Is Now — McEntee emphasized the important election facing the nation:

"At the dawn of the 21st century, we are poised on the brink of major strides for our members and for all working families. If we have the courage and commitment to stay the course and do the hard work ahead, there is a wealth of gains to be realized." Pointing to goals such as universal health care coverage, implementation of paid medical leave and collective bargaining rights for public employees in every state in the nation, he indicated that the nation was ready to take these steps forward.

Months earlier, McEntee had written about this historic moment: "For years, public employees have negotiated with politicians and government managers for wages and benefits in an environment of fiscal challenges. When the economy takes a downturn, the revenues of cities and states suffer... and public employees have been asked and have made personal sacrifices during these tough times. When cities such as New York and Philadelphia have had financial crises, public employees have agreed to minimal raises, and many times no raises, to preserve government services."

As McEntee made clear, the Clinton years brought unparalleled prosperity, building a federal budget surplus while boosting state and local government funding that allowed the most positive economic forecast in over a generation; 44 states were projected to have surpluses. Yet even then, right-wing politicians called for massive tax cuts, rather than rewarding government employees. In one of the most grievous examples, New York's Giuliani spoke of offering public workers zero pay increases despite a 3 billion dollar surplus. McEntee responded: "There is no reason that public service employees should not be sharing in the improved fiscal conditions of jurisdictions all around the country — especially since they have given up so much."

Well before the 2000 Presidential race, Jerry McEntee had placed AFSCME at the center of the early nomination process to determine the Democratic Party's candidate. In 1999, the union polled its members at two regional conferences, revealing a strong consensus among members for Vice President Al Gore. However, New Jersey Senator Bill Bradley was mounting a vigorous challenge, and some within the labor movement wanted to wait to see the results in Iowa and New Hampshire before committing to either candidate.

AFSCME members pushed hard for Gore, believing that the vice-president had a more solid pro-labor history. McEntee, reflecting their view, was direct: "Where I am from, you don't walk out on a friend who has always been there for you just at the point when he needs you. Al Gore has stood by us, and we will stand by him."

McEntee was pivotal in securing the AFL-CIO endorsement for Gore in November, in the belief that coming out early would give the vice-president the needed momentum in the general election. Following the AFL-CIO pronouncement, AFSCME's International Executive Board issued a similar statement in December 1999.

McEntee's support for Gore grew out of the vice-president's strong pro-labor stand. At the 1998 AFSCME Convention,

Gore made his beliefs clear. "AFSCME is leading the way state by state, minute by minute. Your passion and commitment are helping the labor movement to reach its greatest strength in two decades. You are helping all Americans understand a basic truth — that the right to organize is a fundamental American right that can never be blocked, can never be stopped, can never be taken away."

Gore challenged AFSCME members to fight for progressive causes: "Are you willing to match, and more than match, the intensity of right-wing extremists on the other side?" Praising AFSCME's president, Gore went on to say, "Jerry McEntee is never happier than when he is wearing his green T-shirt, raising his voice, fighting for the working families of America and creating positive change."

AFSCME members across the nation agreed with the union's strong stand for Gore. "We had been getting Democrats to understand why union growth was better for them," Booth says. "We even had a verb for it: 'algorizing.' To algorize a candidate, you took them around to organizing drives and you immersed them in it and got them to feel the injustice so many workers face day by day. By the time he was nominated, Al Gore had been thoroughly algorized. He'd been to enough places that he could get up and tell an emotional story about workers. So we figured that winning in 2000 could get us part way to the Promised Land."

Gore's opposition was Texas Governor George W. Bush. That strengthened AFSCME's resolve. Through early 2000, Bush campaigned as a "compassionate conservative," a vague tag that seemed to imply sensitivity to human needs. AFSCME knew he was no moderate. As Texas governor, Bush had supported a range of radical measures, including an attempt to privatize the administration of the state's welfare system, a move that would have threatened the jobs of 13,000 state employees, not to mention the citizens they served. Texas also led the nation in the number of private prisons. He was proudly anti-labor, supporting proposals that would gut union political influence, as well as legislation that would destroy Texas's workers compensation fund and pensions for public employees.

In the midst of this Presidential contest, McEntee oversaw a massive, union-sponsored education of the American electorate. An historic moment was at hand — one in which the nation would decide which of two paths, both formed in the previous twenty years. The choice was to follow Reagan's path of the 1980s or Clinton's path of the 1990s. McEntee put the choice starkly: "There has not been, in my two decades-plus at the head of this union, any election as important as the one we now face."

McEntee had compelling facts to back up his claim. In the 1980s, Americans faced economic devastation, inflation, farm foreclosures and job losses, while AFSCME's members, year after year, were forced to "take zeroes" and reductions in their health care plans. In 1992, AFSCME played a major role in changing the direction that the nation was taking. With the election of Bill Clinton, the country saw 21.6 million new jobs and a $211-billion budget surplus.

The Republican nomination of George W. Bush and Dick Cheney meant a turn away from the policies of the 1990s.

McEntee ticked off their failures: "They represent Big Business, the wealthy, the privileged. They want to build up tax breaks for the rich and hold down unions for working people; roll back civil rights and women's rights by packing the Supreme Court with arch-conservatives; clamp down on the right to organize."

McEntee helped launch the AFL-CIO's Labor 2000 program, a major voter-mobilization drive for pro-labor candidates at both national and local level. Through these grass-roots efforts, 2.3 million new union voters were registered, with 100,000 volunteers marshaled through e-mail to serve at phone banks to support Al Gore and other Democratic Party candidates. AFSCME led all unions in political contributions, which exceeded eight million dollars. Leading up to November, AFSCME brigades appeared behind Gore at almost every campaign stop, and worked in get-out-the-vote efforts.

On Election Day, AFSCME volunteers across the country felt positive that their cause would prevail. That night, many state races resulted in razor-thin margins for one party's candidate or the other's. As news stations tried to make sense of the results, there was confusion over who had gained the necessary electoral votes to attain the victory. With its fine-tuned political apparatus on the ground in Florida, AFSCME leaders kept in touch with McEntee throughout the evening. Those with the clearest understanding asserted that Gore would take the state. Recalling this historic night, McEntee stated emphatically: "Gore really won Florida. The night of the election, as results were coming in, Bill Daley, Gore's campaign manager, called me and said they had agreed to recount something like six counties in Florida. He said, 'Jerry, we got it, because these six counties are ours.'"

"I replied, 'Let me tell you something, Bill. If you think they are going to let you count those six counties — we can't be the only ones who know they're ours, okay? You've got to make the position known that you are going to demand a recount of all the counties, all right? Count them all or count none.'"

Travelling in his motorcade, Gore — believing he had narrowly lost — called Bush to concede the election. Minutes later, McEntee, having heard that Gore had given up, called him. "I told him, 'Don't you give up. You haven't lost, man, don't you do that.'" Gore then called Bush to take back his concession.

In the ensuing recount, both the Democratic and Republican parties maneuvered to secure the election for their candidate. AFSCME played a crucial role in this struggle. In the words of one staff member, "We were absolutely obsessed with the Florida recount." McEntee placed hundreds of staff, local officers and member activists there and in the nation's capital, organizing rallies to pressure for a full, state-wide recount. Observing how the union came together to fight in this crucial moment in the nation's history, Legislative Director Chuck Loveless points to McEntee's leadership and his refusal to quit. "That's how he is, he goes for broke."

In his own analysis, McEntee continues to believe that a full recount was needed for democracy to have functioned in the

2000 race. "We would have won the damned thing down there — but they didn't do it." The result remains a blemish on the nation's history.

17

Struggling Through Destruction and Death

A year later, a very different kind of crisis erupted. On September 11, 2001, terrorists attacked the World Trade Center and the Pentagon, and downed an additional airliner in Pennsylvania. Father Mychal F. Judge, a New York Fire Department chaplain and a member of AFSCME Local 299 (DC 37), was among the first to arrive at the scene in New York. Father Judge did not hesitate when he heard of the attacks. He put on his collar and went to be of help. He died giving the Last Rites of the Roman Catholic Church to a mortally wounded firefighter. He is known today as the Saint of 9/11.

Father Judge was not alone. Paramedics Carlos Lillo and Ricardo Quinn, both DC 37 members, braved the horrors in Lower Manhattan to support rescue efforts. They, too, gave their lives, as did Chet Louie, an AFSCME member who worked a second job at the World Trade Center, and five members of the Civil Service Employees Association (CSEA)/ AFSCME Local 1000 — Yvette Anderson, Florence Cohen, Harry Goody, Marian Hrycak and Dorothy Temple — who worked for the state Department of Taxation and Finance in the South Tower.

Sixty-nine paramedics and emergency technicians were injured, in addition to countless others who worked in the buildings. Unable to bring stretchers into the building, emergency workers brought the injured out by carrying them over their shoulders. Thirty ambulances were destroyed. On that day and in the months and years that followed, AFSCME members worked to save and rebuild New York City.

Lee Saunders, who was still overseeing operations at DC 37, was two blocks from the World Trade Center. "My apartment was right across the street," Saunders recalled. "I would walk the catwalk over the West Side Highway to the Trade Center to get to our building every day." September 11 was primary day in New York City, and union staff was already dispersed across the city. Saunders was driving across the Brooklyn Bridge when the second plane hit.

DC 37 had a campaign called Everyday Heroes, putting posters and ads on buses and subways to remind the public of the important work AFSCME members do in the everyday life of the city. That was clearly evident on this tragic day. "People saw the value of public service," Saunders remembers. "We didn't have people running from Ground Zero. We had people running to it."

AFSCME members responded immediately. Those who worked in cafeterias travelled to Ground Zero to pass out food to the rescuers. Members were there every day during the weeks following the attack. Responding to the urgent need facing their brothers and sisters, CSEA members raised $16,000 in a few hours. President McEntee, in a call to Saunders shortly after the attack, told him to "Do whatever you have to do. You've got the full support of the International union."

McEntee visited New York's AFSCME members and staff and held an emotional meeting with them at a midtown hotel. In a statement of solidarity with all New Yorkers, he ordered AFSCME's national Women's Conference, which was scheduled to be held in Boston, moved to New York City. And the union declared in an official statement, "With this new sense of respect and solidarity, now is the time for AFSCME and other unions to go forth and make sure all workers are treated fairly. Now is the time to get decent wages, decent health care benefits, retirement benefits, job security and job safety for these 21st century heroes."

After the terrorist attacks, AFSCME set up the September 11 Relief Fund to assist members who were directly affected by the tragedy, raising more than $800,000 in donations. For Sadig Rasool, a member of Local 1407 (DC 37), AFSCME's aid was "generous and timely." He lost his wife, Amenia, who worked at the World Trade Center. She left behind four very young children, including one only six months old.

Lena Dawson, a member of Local 372 (DC 37), whose husband was killed that day, said the fund provided her family with "some financial security and stability. AFSCME's help — which I never expected — provided a strong boost emotionally."

In the years that followed, McEntee and AFSCME continued the efforts to help victims of the 9/11 attacks — as well as AFSCME members who lost their lives fighting in Iraq and Afghanistan, and those who faced hardships after natural disasters such as Hurricane Katrina and other violent storms. The Fallen Heroes Fund has raised hundreds of thousands of dollars for union members and their families after disasters. McEntee has regularly asked his former special assistant, Gloria T. Caoile, to coordinate AFSCME's response to tornados, floods and the like.

In 2002, wiht AFSCME's backing, Congress passed legislation named for Father Judge. The Mychal Judge Police and Fire Chaplains Public Safety Officers' Benefit Act provides a $250,000 payment to families of firefighters, law enforcement and corrections officers, and emergency-response workers killed in the line of duty.

18

Challenging Bush

Progressives looked to the 2004 election as a way to remedy the political direction in which the country was headed and to rectify the erroneous — if not "stolen" — election of 2000. As he had in elections since 1992, McEntee brought AFSCME's power into play in the early selection process of Democratic candidates. As the field of candidates took shape, no one candidate stood out. The Teamsters were backing Dick Gephardt, whose strong labor record made him appealing.

McEntee and Gephardt were close allies, but AFSCME's leadership knew that Gephardt had no operation and that his campaign wasn't going anywhere. Further, his voting record, although good for labor, was not necessarily good for getting elected. Some in labor had begun to take a serious look at North Carolina Senator John Edwards, while the International Association of Firefighters was strongly backing Massachusetts Senator John Kerry. Vermont's progressive former governor, Howard Dean, was also running and looking for labor support. Going into the last months of 2003, AFSCME had yet to endorse a candidate.

Although an endorsement decision would be made by the IEB and the delegates at the upcoming AFSCME Convention, McEntee met with his top members of his staff to discuss the candidates.

McEntee asked, "Who should we endorse?"

Larry Scanlon said, "Edwards."

McEntee replied, "No, he's off the table." McEntee had first met Edwards four years earlier, and had come away unimpressed. He asked his political director for a different candidate. "Who do you want?"

"Edwards," Scanlon said again.

"Weren't you listening to me? Edwards is out of the picture. Of the remaining candidates?"

"Dean seems to have the best shot," was the reply.

McEntee was open to the possibility of backing Dean, a physician who understood the medical field and was deeply committed to comprehensive health care reform legislation. Around the country, Dean was gaining an enthusiastic following and lots of young volunteers with his strong opposition to the Iraq war. His campaign was also getting attention for the ways in which it was using the Internet to mobilize supporters.

AFSCME's IEB came out for Dean by the end of the year, and union members aggressively campaigned for him in the early contests. Facing a bruising campaign in Iowa, his standing began to drop as John Kerry gained ground. Dean finished a disappointing third, and his election night speech — punctuated by a screaming yell — further harmed his chances. After hearing the speech on early morning television broadcasts, AFSCME's leaders knew the Vermonter was doomed.

McEntee recalled, "If our people aren't going to support him, he's dead in the water." The time had come to end the union's support. McEntee flew to Vermont to meet with the governor at his campaign headquarters to break the news to him in person. With McEntee was SEIU President Andy Stern, who planned to say something similar. When they met, McEntee was immediate and blunt: "Look, we're done. We're not going to back you any further."

Dean was emphatic that his national campaign could regain momentum. But McEntee held firm: "We're not with you." AFSCME's backing of the Dean campaign was over.

Through the primary season, John Kerry continued to pull in victories, and quickly emerged as the Democratic Party's nominee. AFSCME came out for the senator, mobilizing thousands of members and pledging millions of dollars to the campaign. Despite the strong support, Kerry was narrowly defeated in November 2004. Again, the election of George W. Bush bode poorly for American workers, who faced more difficult organizing environments across the nation as well as a federal Labor Department that placed business concerns over those of workers.

"We had absolutely no relationship whatsoever with the Bush administration," Legislative Director Chuck Loveless recalls. Such a difficult political environment put severe limitations on the kinds of measures McEntee hoped to see enacted after 2004. Even worse, the union would need to combat some of the most radical conservative initiatives in the nation's history.

The start of George W. Bush's second term in office graphically illustrated the fundamental difference between progressives and conservatives over the direction the nation should take. Nothing made this clearer than Bush's effort to dismantle the Social Security program. Understanding the impact this would have on millions of retirees and seniors across the land, AFSCME mobilized to thwart the Bush attempt to put Social Security into Wall Street's hands.

In 2005, McEntee helped form Americans United to Protect Social Security, which brought together 200 progressive organizations motivated by their members' realization of the importance of Social Security in their own lives. "Privatization will amount to gambling with the accounts," said Joseph Overton, a former social service worker for the city of Philadelphia and a District Council 47 retiree. "The average Joe, who is not savvy, can lose their life savings" with private retirement accounts invested in the stock market.

With Americans United, AFSCME organized hundreds of grass-roots events and rallies across the country. No other organization was as effective in this struggle. In 2005, when President Bush announced a "60 cities in 60 days tour" to promote his plan, AFSCME decided to meet him at every stop he made. "He said he was going to roll back Social Security, so we followed him," McEntee remembered. "We beat the hell out of him, man. All over the place. It got so bad he went to only a few states, and in each state he visited, his position on Social Security went down and so did his popularity. He quit going places."

When objections arose to Bush using government money for his anti-Social Security campaign, AFSCME stuck a rhetorical knife into him. McEntee sent Bush a letter saying the union would provide the money so he could go to the rest of the states to plead his case. There was no response.

The opposition of AFSCME and Americans United to the Bush plan was crucial to the plan's defeat. Chuck Loveless says of this particular struggle: "Bush never got his mojo back after that. We were able to shift the discussion; there was much more opposition to Bush, it showed he wasn't invincible. I think we emboldened his opponents." With this victory at the national level secured, AFSCME went on to challenge California Governor Arnold Schwarzenegger's effort to privatize the existing state employee pension fund with a 401(k) style-plan.

The battle to preserve Social Security helped secure AFSCME's reputation as one of the nation's strongest voices for progressive causes. Bush's privatization campaign, in addition to his poor handling of the federal response to Hurricane Katrina, had weakened his Presidency. National polls recorded a severe decline in his approval.

McEntee once again helped craft the political approach leading up to the 2006 congressional elections. He believed they offered a key opportunity to take power out of the hands of the nation's most conservative bloc. At the federal level, AFSCME's political program mobilized thousands and was instrumental in taking back the House in 2006, gaining 30 seats there and six in the Senate. In state elections, Democrats took back six governorships from Republicans and now held a gubernatorial majority across the nation. Democrats also made gains in ten state legislative houses.

Soon another historic — and to AFSCME important — development unfolded: the election of California Rep. Nancy Pelosi as the first woman Speaker of the House. McEntee first met Pelosi in 1989, when Senator Alan Cranston of California introduced them at a football game. AFSCME had supported her first run for Congress two years earlier, when she faced a tough race to fill the seat of the late Sala Burton. Over the years since their meeting, Pelosi had become a close friend of Jerry and Barbara McEntee.

Pelosi had earned a reputation as one of the most progressive members of the House, supporting AFSCME's political program in all areas. Speaking at union headquarters shortly after her election as Speaker of the House, she noted that "We would not have won this election without you being everywhere we faced a challenge. Without your help, we would not have won the majority. I have no better friend in labor than AFSCME."

During her years as speaker, Pelosi secured passage of legislation providing more than $250 billion in assistance for state and local governments, in addition to landmark legislation such as health care reform, Wall Street reform and tax cuts for the middle class. "We supported her whenever and wherever we could, when legislation was tough on the Hill," McEntee notes. "And she supported us. Even when it was difficult, she was right there. She came to all of our rallies, came to all of our Conventions, wherever we asked. In my judgment, the best member of Congress for working people has been Nancy Pelosi."

The election of Nancy Pelosi as Speaker also marks a significant gender shift in the American political order. A result of the women's movement of the last half of the 20th century, increasing numbers of women have attained positions of power in Washington and in state and municipal legislatures around the country. Such advancements were seen in all levels of society, as women took more visible positions in news media and other areas — and within AFSCME. In 1962, women accounted for only 19 percent of union membership in the United States. By the early 21st century, the number was up to 43 percent — and to 56 percent in AFSCME.

McEntee had always understood the importance of union membership for women. Those who belong to unions earn 35 percent more money than those who do not, and the differential is more than salary alone. It also means having a greater chance for employer-sponsored health and disability services. McEntee insured that AFSCME took the lead in the labor movement by developing programs that focused on the needs of women. He expanded the Women's Advisory Committee and the scheduling of regular women's conferences — initiatives launched during Jerry Wurf's presidency — at which activists from across the country could share ideas and develop new strategies. Advancing basic workplace rights for American women placed AFSCME on the front lines of gender equality.

19

Blending Old and New Methods for a New Age

The age of the Internet and the emergence of cable news channels transformed the political landscape, allowing instant transmittal of information, and interconnecting activists in ways never before imagined. Technological changes came to everyday life — with information technology in laptop and personal computers, e-mail, the blogosphere, cell phones and smartphones. Once again, AFSCME took the lead.

McEntee began to blog on sites such as Huffington Post and Firedoglake. In 1996, AFCSME developed and introduced its own website, one of the first labor unions in the nation to do so. Other AFSCME innovations included a "Legislative Action" link developed for the website. Routinely, at legislative and regional conferences, the union's members were mobilized on the spot to make phone calls to legislators and rally fellow members to do the same — a model that has been adopted across the labor movement.

Ongoing member outreach and education remain at the heart of these efforts. AFSCME established an innovative Leadership Academy to continue the union's emphasis on education, overseeing training from everything from organizing to auditing, while using new technology to bring it to members across the nation.

With McEntee's full support, AFSCME invested in other "technologies of democracy." The union created an in-house phone-banking system to help keep in touch with members. It expanded the use of video, and made aggressive efforts to attract members and the general public through Facebook and Twitter. By 2012, AFSCME was the most popular union on both of those social media. In 2011, it was using them to mobilize members and allies in the critical battles the union faced during the brutal battles in Wisconsin, Ohio and other battleground states.

AFSCME also relies on older forms of political empowerment — sometimes in new ways. One innovative plan begun in 2005 has been the AFSCME-funded Congressional Boot Camp project, launched in 2005 by Christine Pelosi. The boot camp offers Congressional candidates leadership seminars, regional roundtables and virtual trainings showcasing the best practices and lessons learned in management, messaging and mobilization. The program has proved successful: so far, 12 graduates have been elected to Congress.

Faced with the growing right-wing challenge to public services, McEntee pressed for a top-to-bottom reassessment of how AFSCME functions. In 2004, delegates at the AFSCME International Convention passed a resolution "calling on our union to examine itself from top to bottom and recommend bold changes."

Across the country, the union solicited members' ideas through online surveys and national and regional conferences, and town hall gatherings in local unions and councils. During this time, McEntee set up AFSCME's Twenty-first Century Committee. Leaders across the country formulated a set of goals that involved higher standards, higher dues and higher expectations for what councils could do, and the goals were adopted at the 2006 International Convention. Power to Win, as the program was called, is grounded on a basic strategic principle: the union is stronger when it has a large, active and growing membership with real political power. Power to Win has six main priorities: build more member participation; elect pro-worker politicians and hold them accountable; increase AFSCME's membership; expand union-building capacity; win high-quality, affordable health care; and project a bold image for our union while promoting public services.

"When the 2006 Convention voted for Power to Win, they authorized new resources for a stronger political-action program," notes McEntee. "They voted to strengthen our council and local union structures, while mobilizing broader and deeper member activism."

Larry Scanlon places this in context, explaining of McEntee: "Here's a guy who's been in charge for many years, and he says let's do a top-to-bottom review of how we do things. It takes a lot of courage to do that because you are giving up a measure of control." Lee Saunders also points to this initiative as an important illustration of McEntee's confidence as a leader: "We went through a very exhaustive process about the direction this union needs to take. It showed again not only Jerry's ability to lead, but also the importance of listening to other folks."

Through these important transitional moments, McEntee developed a different philosophy for how the national union apparatus would function. Watching this change in union culture, Paul Booth notes: "In significant ways, he demanded a raise in the caliber of different departments, breaking down turf to make everyone function more as a team. We have a pretty high degree of teamwork, and are able to carry out a vision."

The union's youth program, the Next Wave, emerged from the grassroots and McEntee quickly embraced it. Envisioned by sections of young AFSCME members — with original sections coming together in Oregon, Pennsylvania and Washington state — the Next Wave aims to bring workers 35 years and younger into closer association with the union, through social and mentoring programs.

AFSCME's focus on internal mentoring and youth leadership has become a model for at the labor movement. In 2010, the AFL-CIO initiated its own youth program, hosting the Next Up Young Workers Summit in Washington.

Dave Levine of AFSCME Local 2577 (Council 13), a clerk typist with the Pennsylvania Department of Welfare, was one of many AFSCME activists represented at the second Next Up Conference in October 2011. Levine says, "This year's summit provided an opportunity to continue conversations begun last summer between young workers across the labor movement, to see how far we've come since and to come up with new, creative ideas on how we can work together on issues that affect not only public employees but all of labor."

20

The 2008 Election

Democratic legislative victories in 2006 seemed to point to further AFSCME successes in the 2008 elections. Leading up to the party's primaries, McEntee again placed AFSCME and the union's members at the center of the process for selecting a successful Presidential candidate. Even more than in previous years, AFSCME's trademark green seemed an ever-present element of the nation's political landscape. In 2007, Senator Harry Reid asked McEntee to put together the first Presidential candidate forum. He wanted it to be in Nevada. McEntee worked to schedule a forum in Carson City, hosted by George Stephanopoulos of ABC News.

In the Nevada debate, and at a subsequent forum moderated by Chris Matthews and televised on MSNBC, AFSCME was front and center in electoral politics. But once again, McEntee wanted to be sure that the membership had a voice. Leading up to the election cycle, he initiated a vigorous process of polling AFSCME members. More than 45,000 responded to the survey, indicating a clear choice of Hillary Clinton.

Clinton's wisdom in understanding the national political system, especially her detailed experience in trying to pass major health care reform with her husband in 1993, made her an appealing candidate. Having been through the flak of right-wing political attacks, she had also proven herself a tough fighter. After AFSCME's International Executive Board endorsed Clinton in October 2007, McEntee provided her with a pair of boxing gloves — a photo of which appeared on the front page of *The New York Times*.

Throughout the first half of 2008, AFSCME placed its full support behind Clinton, with green Hillary signs and T-shirts becoming standard at almost every campaign stop and speech. McEntee often appeared with Clinton or teamed up with her husband to urge primary voters to support the former First Lady. While other strong unions, including the American Federation of Teachers, gave their support to Clinton, none outdid AFSCME, which poured seven or eight million dollars into her campaign.

Nevada emerged as a major battleground. Just before caucus day there, the powerful HERE union known as the Las Vegas Culinary Workers came out for Illinois Senator Barack Obama. Many pundits believed that sealed the election, with caucus sites established on the main casino strip to assure maximum participation from these workers. Undaunted, AFSCME pressed on with an aggressive effort that took the fight for Hillary Clinton right to the heart of the Culinary Workers' seat of power.

On caucus day, AFSCME organizers went into the hotels and casinos to lobby workers to come out for Hillary. McEntee himself sought opportunities to meet with the hotel workers throughout the day. "We were all assigned different hotel casinos to campaign for Hillary. I had the Paris. I talked to the people who cleaned the hotel rooms. I would talk to everybody about Hillary Clinton. Most people didn't give Hillary a chance because the Culinary Workers had endorsed Obama."

On caucus day, Bill Clinton and McEntee campaigned together — "in the kitchens and all over that damned place. Clinton did a great job. He talked to everybody." Hillary Clinton won all but one of the hotel and casino caucuses on the Las Vegas main strip, and won the state of Nevada.

After one of the longest primary-election seasons in history, Hillary Clinton ended her campaign and called for party unity. After her concession, AFSCME's IEB endorsed Senator Obama. "Barack Obama has mobilized a historic movement to reclaim the greatness of America," McEntee declared in his statement. "With his leadership, our nation will rise up to rebuild the middle class at home, and restore America's reputation in the world."

During the Presidential campaign, AFSCME's Green Machine went into full operation, with thousands of volunteers logging more than 4.3 million phone calls to members, mobilizing 40,000 activists along with more than 500 staff, and placing $67 million behind Obama's effort. The AFL-CIO political program that McEntee had developed sent 250,000 union volunteers into action, combining cutting-edge voter communications with massive grassroots strength. "Our people created the largest, most efficient independent voter-mobilization initiative in American history," McEntee notes.

Among union households in battleground states, there was clear momentum for Obama on the eve of the election. What moved people? "The issues, and talking to workers one on one," McEntee says. For example, in Pennsylvania, polls showed Barack Obama gained 22 percent after August for a 67-27 percent advantage going into Election Day.

When Obama was elected the 44th President of the United States, McEntee saw "a mandate for building an America that lives up to its ideals. As we celebrate this victory, we also face monumental challenges as a country. Working families are ready to join with President-elect Obama to meet these challenges and enact a bold agenda for change."

21

Years of Challenge and Hope

Barack Obama's victory obliged him to cope with the most dangerous economic crisis the nation had faced since the Great Depression. With the world's economic system teetering on collapse due to irresponsible practices of a deregulated financial industry, millions of average Americans faced long-term unemployment and the loss of their homes. The American auto industry was sounding a death knell, a loss that would have worsened the blow to the fragile economy. In this fearful climate, McEntee called for AFSCME members to get behind a Make America Happen initiative — a political project that prioritized goals such as the revitalization of the economy through an extensive recovery package and affordable health care for all.

AFSCME channeled the union's power to help President Obama pass the American Recovery and Reinvestment Act, with a federal investment of $282 billion in public services

— including billions in direct local aid to states, townships and cities — to create and save jobs. The money helped stabilize hard-pressed state and local governments — and, in the process kept thousands of AFSCME members employed through a time of uncertainty. Following the bill's narrow passage, President Obama personally called McEntee to thank AFSCME for its support.

McEntee then turned his attention to comprehensive health care reform legislation. From the start of the health care legislative process, AFSCME was involved at the highest level. "We played a major role," AFSCME Legislative Director Chuck Loveless recalls. "We had daily meetings with many members of Congress and key senators to push the bill forward." Other AFSCME officials did the same. McEntee's participation was especially useful because he had learned much from his earlier experience in trying to pass the Clinton's health bill in the early 1990s. He had also served on the Health Care Commission designed to protect consumers against excessive charges by the health care industry.

McEntee believed that the 1993 measure had failed largely because it had come from the top down, taking shape behind closed doors and without sufficient Congressional input. Union efforts to bring the new bill to American communities began even before the 2008 election. In 2007, McEntee launched a coalition called Health Care for America Now (HCAN), which included eighty labor, community, online, health activist, women's and other groups. HCAN trained community activists to understand all aspects of the plan and to serve as "Truth Tellers" in open debates with political officials and fellow citizens.

AFSCME also bolstered existing groups committed to improved health care, including the Maine People's Alliance. That action, in a state with limited union power, proved critical in convincing Republican lawmakers to support the reforms. In addition, the union sent a "Highway to Health Care" bus to ten states and twenty cities in the month when debate over the law was reaching its peak.

Through this process, McEntee worked behind the scenes, making repeated trips to the White House. He recalls one meeting that went all night long, from six at night until six in the morning. At one critical moment, some Democratic leaders agreed to a provision in the proposed law that would tax union health-care plans, a measure unacceptable to McEntee and other national labor leaders. In emergency meetings with key Democrats, McEntee made his case that failure to change the proposed taxes would result in the union's backing away from the legislation. "Do you want us to spend all our time fighting you on this issue?" McEntee asked. "Don't you need us out there doing everything we need to push health care reform?" The provision was modified.

The health care campaign produced the largest mobilization around a single issue in AFSCME history, with more than 250,000 phone calls, letters and emails to Congress. McEntee authorized an unprecedented advertising campaign, including a national television spot featuring AFSCME nurses. AFSCME Retirees spread the message to tens of thousands of retired union members in targeted states.

With the passage of health care reform, McEntee noted the many positive changes that would stem from the law. "This victory will protect and improve good union health-care benefits," he said. "It stops the worst abuses of the insurance companies. It gives workers and families without coverage on-the-job access to affordable health care. It ends skyrocketing premiums and caps on benefits. It helps seniors by strengthening Medicare and helps preserve employer coverage for early retirees. It provides critical new funding to states."

But he recognized that more help was needed for working families. Too many Americans were struggling to cope in the worst economy since the Great Depression. State and local governments continued to cut services to the bone. And things were going to get even more difficult in the months to come.

22

Building a Main Street Movement

In 2011, for the first time, membership in public sector unions represented a majority of union members in the United States. The vision and determination that Jerry McEntee had brought to AFSCME had given 1.6 million AFSCME members and their families better lives, and boosted conditions and opportunities for millions of additional working men and women. Millions of Americans regard the union's successes as essential in advancing a progressive vision for the nation in the 21st century.

Many others, however, saw AFSCME as a major threat to corporate dominance of U.S. society. Powerful right-wing forces sought to silence working Americans, and targeted AFSCME in the belief that weakening public sector unions is required for them to enact their agenda. The 2010 elections gave them an opportunity. Republicans took control of the House of Representatives as Tea Party candidates won victories throughout the country. At the state level, the right wing pulled off a "trifecta" in 17 states, gaining control of the governor's office and both houses of the state legislature. McEntee saw threats to collective bargaining, political check-off and the retirement security of AFSCME members. Further, he considered the threat of privatization greater than at any time in the past: "We faced opposition from Republicans, and even some Democrats were laying down markers."

To meet those challenges, he oversaw a response that had a scale and intensity much greater than any effort AFSCME had mounted previously. The union created Battleground State Partnerships, a Privatization Action Center, an energized Rapid Response Program, and a Stop the Lies Campaign to help mobilize members and allies to overcome the threats. "We saw a real need for comprehensive campaigns," McEntee says. "So we created them, including member mobilization programs, earned and paid media, grassroots lobbying, and better coordination with other unions and coalition partners."

The first weeks of 2011 would prove to be among the most difficult in the union's history. With right-wing gains throughout the country in 2010, most understood that the nation's unions, especially in the public sector, would face challenges. Yet few believed that the measures proposed by Republican governors and law makers would be as radical as they turned out to be. In February, in Wisconsin, recently elected Republican Governor Scott Walker announced a Draconian measure aimed at eliminating collective bargaining rights for nearly 200,000 Wisconsin public state service employees, including 60,000 AFSCME members. Walker's push to destroy AFSCME in his state came as a surprise: he had not campaigned on the issue. His sudden attack against public workers was a coordinated attempt to break the union and — the fact that it happened in the state where AFSCME had been founded gave the assault an obvious symbolic quality.

McEntee understood Walker's action as nothing short of an attack against the union's existence. Just days later, Ohio Republican Governor John Kasich called for legislation to rescind the bargaining rights of the state's 350,000 public employees. Immediately, McEntee promised to fight the proposals. He mobilized the union's national staff to begin coordinating solidarity actions with AFSCME chapters in Wisconsin and across the country. The movement that emerged in just a matter of days produced some of the most dramatic displays of worker unity in living memory.

"I'm here to protect my rights as a worker, to have a seat at the bargaining table, and for my kids and their kids," said Adam Sutter, a corrections officer from Prairie du Chien, Wisconsin "I told my children we are a movement, we are making history." Tens of thousands of union members and supporters came to Madison in a massive show of solidarity, holding a round-the-clock-vigil inside Wisconsin's state capitol. Democratic legislators left the state to prevent the quorum required to enact the proposed law.

Madison became the epicenter of a movement to protect the nation's middle class. Covered extensively on national and international news outlets, the protest inspired an outpouring of web-based solidarity actions around the world. Supporters from around the United States joined public workers and their families in displays of unity. Speaking in the cold in Madison, Wisconsin, in February 2011, McEntee declared, "We're not going to be quiet when politicians would try to ram through a bill that would deny our God-given rights — we're not going to be silent when politicians tell us that silence is the only option and that negotiations are part of the past. I say: Bullshit!"

With AFSCME sponsorship, broad coalitions emerged under the banner "We Are Wisconsin!" and "We Are Ohio!" bringing together union members, parents, schoolteachers and students, retirees and taxpayers to stand up to arch-conservative lawmakers. During these struggles, it was revealed that many anti-labor legislators, as well as Walker and Kasich and other anti-union governors, were funded by billionaires David and Charles Koch, whose radical right-wing agenda seeks to eliminate any union presence in the United States. Through 2011, AFSCME's top executive repeatedly issued statements to make the nation aware of the forces at work behind such radical legislation.

At the same time, McEntee oversaw a massive effort to strengthen the ability of AFSCME members to combat the threats. The union created a "Faces and Voices" program to put members out front, giving them the training needed for public speaking and effective media appearances. Union leaders scheduled a record number of conferences, including a Pension Summit and a State Battles Summit, along with large gatherings of AFSCME women, nurses, public safety employees and Next Wavers, to give leaders and activists an opportunity to share experiences and best practices.

McEntee called the engaged response of union members and other activists "a Main Street movement." What began in rallies in Madison and Columbus expanded throughout the country and helped to inspire Occupy Wall Street, which brought greater attention to the concerns of what was being called the 99%. "We worked to combine the power of our members with the whole labor movement and with allies throughout the country," McEntee notes. "It made a difference."

Through a series of recall elections in Wisconsin in August of 2011, AFSCME and its allies were able to deny Governor Walker a working Senate majority in Wisconsin. They made plans to recall the governor himself. In Ohio, voters, in a citizens' veto in the fall, overwhelmingly rejected Governor Kasich's plan to eliminate public employee collective-bargaining rights. "We delivered a clear message to corporate-backed politicians across the country that we will no longer stay silent as Wall Street tries to steal the American Dream," McEntee told the press. "We sent a message to all politicians to end the attacks on the economic and retirement security of the working middle class."

In the course of these fights, AFSCME members discovered that many other citizens were committed to the fight for public services. The union sought to build on these developments, organizing larger coalitions to fight back against budget cutbacks, privatization plans and cuts in benefits. As the union celebrated its 75th anniversary, AFSCME members across the country pulled together to fight with renewed spirit. "We have sharpened our message, built broader unity and deepened the level of our members' activism," McEntee said with satisfaction. "We will continue to take the lead."

On November 3, 2011, McEntee announced that he would not be a candidate for president of the union at its Convention in 2012. After 56 years as an AFSCME member and 31 years as president, he told the union's members that "I have never been more confident in our ability to rally the American people. When we pull together and are united in a fight, nobody can defeat us. When we fight, we win. And when we win, the lives of working people in this country improve."

Later in the month, he gave an interview that would be included in a video commemorating the union's 75th anniversary. He recalled the great battles in AFSCME's past and spoke of his long record of service. As the taping came to an end, he expressed his belief that AFSCME would continue to be a powerful force in the creation of a nation where every citizen can have a voice in the corridors of power: "I will always be proud of the work we have done and the obstacles we have conquered during these past decades of opportunity and challenge."

He closed with this thought: "People like myself, presidents and officials, they come and go, but the union institutionally stays and stays and stays."

23

The End of an Era

On December 6, 2011, AFSCME endorsed Barack Obama for a second term as President of the United States. The vote by the International Executive Board was unanimous. "We must put people back to work, make the 1% pay their fair share, and protect Medicaid, Medicare and Social Security," McEntee said. "President Obama will stand up for working families, but the GOP candidates just don't get it. They are out of touch with reality."

The challenges would go on. After 31 years at the helm of the most powerful union in America — a union that he had forged into a strong Green Machine — this was the last Presidential endorsement McEntee would ever make.

One day later, as a driving rain fell along the east coast of the United States, hundreds of working men and women, leaders from the labor movement, AFSCME IEB members,

Senators and congressmen, along with friends and family members, gathered in Washington to celebrate the career and contributions of Gerald W. McEntee.

There were nurses and EMTs, correction officers and secretaries, along with health care and home care workers. These were the people for whom McEntee had fought to give a voice. They were joined by firefighters, teachers, federal employees and allies who had stood side by side with him during the difficult decades when his leadership offered hope.

And there were the candidates for whom he had fought over the decades, including Steny Hoyer of Maryland, Lynn Woolsey and Howard Berman of California, Bill Halter of Arkansas, Claire McCaskill of Missouri, Tom Udall of New Mexico, Dale Kildee of Michigan, Frank Lautenberg of New Jersey, Chuck Schumer and Carolyn Maloney of New York, Chaka Fattah of Pennsylvania, Dennis Kucinich of Ohio, Tom Harkin and Bonnie Campbell of Iowa, Jim McDermott of Washington. Secretary of State Hillary Clinton sent a special greeting, as did Maryland Governor Martin O'Malley.

The event, held at the Pan-American Union Headquarters, two blocks from the White House, was organized by Working America, the community-based affiliate of the AFL-CIO, which McEntee had helped to create in the 1990s and had led ever since. The party was far from lavish — Philadelphia cheesesteaks, hoagies, soft pretzels and Tastykakes.

It was to be, at his direction, the only event in his honor.

McEntee and his wife Barbara were joined by their extended family, including his daughters Patty Gehlen, Kelly Hamlin, Chris Serenelli and Kathy Hammock. With them were some of Jerry's grandchildren, Dillon Young, Tyler and Trevor Sernelli, and Luke Hammock. McEntee's sister, Mary Casale along with her son, Bill Casale and his wife, Jessica were there as well.

Actress Maria Bello, a Philadelphia native, came to be a part of the celebration, along with the legendary Philadelphia Eagles wide receiver, Mike Quick, who expressed surprise that so many Philadelphians had driven along I-95 through the downpour to be with McEntee on this special night. "I didn't expect to see so many familiar faces," he told a member of the AFSCME staff. Sha Na Na entertained, along with a group of Mummers from his hometown.

The heartfelt tributes given to McEntee throughout the evening demonstrated the many ways the AFSCME leader has helped American workers and AFSCME's members throughout the years.

One labor leader highlighted how McEntee had helped her understand the challenges that existed in the changing political world. Randi Weingarten of the American Federation of Teachers said that "the reason this union sister is here is to pay homage." Weingarten described a phone call she received from McEntee after her election as AFT president two years earlier:

"'Come to my office.' It wasn't much more than that."

When she arrived for her appointment, McEntee, she said, "sat there, feet on the table.

"He said: 'Kid, what are you going to do? Are you going to be just a teacher type? Or are you going to be a worker type?'

"And frankly," Weingarten recalled, "given what has happened in the last two years, that question was more prescient than anyone would have known in 2008 and 2009.

"What Jerry McEntee and AFSCME have helped build is a workers movement. What AFSCME did was create the muscle for the public sector. What AFSCME did was say that the public sector was part of the big labor movement that fights for others.

"Thanks to Jerry McEntee," she told the crowd, public sector workers are "an incredibly important bridge" in creating "a real social contract of retirement security, and health security and great wages" for all American workers.

"You have built an amazing union," Weingarten told McEntee. "You have led us in an amazing way."

John Sweeney welcomed McEntee to the ranks of retirees, saying: "As someone who has been retired for some time now, Jerry, it's a great life." He recalled McEntee's leadership in reviving the labor movement in the 1990s and said: "For nearly 60 years, Jerry McEntee has supercharged the labor movement with his personality and kept the heart of the progressive movement alive and pumping with his persistence."

House Democratic leader Nancy Pelosi called McEntee a great American and praised the difference he has made for our country. "I worship at the shrine of Jerry McEntee," she said. "Working families across our country are better off because of you."

She thanked public employees for all they have done to strengthen the middle class, and credited McEntee for his help in passing health care reform, pay equity, consumer-protection legislation and the repeal of Don't Ask, Don't Tell. "You are a leader in re-igniting the American Dream," she told McEntee.

Senate Majority Leader Harry Reid quoted Martin Luther King Jr.'s remark that organized labor was "the principal force that transformed misery and despair into hope and progress." And for three decades, he continued, "Jerry McEntee has been a leader in the quest for that progress."

"At the helm of AFSCME," Reid said, "Jerry advocated for every piece of progressive legislation passed in the last three decades. The organization and dedication of Jerry and his 1.6 million brothers and sisters has been invaluable, whether we were raising the minimum wage or passing the Affordable Care Act.

"The labor movement is better because of Jerry. America is a better place because of Jerry."

As the program came to a close, the celebrants saw President Obama on a large screen at the front of the room. He, too, had a message for Jerry McEntee: "I know first-hand that when it comes to standing up for working families, you and AFSCME never give up, and you never give in. Over the years, you've led the fight against the efforts to privatize Social Security, you've helped guarantee equal pay for equal work and made health care reform a reality. And last month, you helped preserve collective bargaining rights in Ohio." That victory, the President noted, "gave working men and working women everywhere a win.

"So Jerry, you've earned your retirement."

President Obama asked the assembled crowd to not give up "until we get every American back to work and rebuild an America that works for every American. We need this country to be a place where responsibility matters. Where if you work hard, you can get ahead; where no matter who you are, you can make it if you try.

"Jerry," the President continued, "I know those are the values you've been fighting for your entire life. That's how you built Working America and AFSCME into such an important force for change, and that's why we cannot rest — not until every American who wants a job can get one and every worker who wants to join a union can do so."

It was a long journey from Swampoodle to that moment. But it was a journey that McEntee had loved, every inch of the way. Unlike so many, he had never forgotten from where he came.

As the festively costumed Mummers, down from the City of Brotherly Love, marched their way through the crowd,

McEntee danced with his grandchildren and called out greetings to friends who caught his eye.

He had fought the good fight. He had kept the faith.

His heart was full.

It was a heart that had helped organize, energize and mobilize AFSCME, the greatest union America has ever known.

It was a heart that had pumped energy into the progressive movement for more than half a century. It was a heart that embraced all working Americans.

It was a heart that had fought to protect and preserve the middle class and the American Dream. It was a heart that had changed America.

It was a rare heart. But everyone in AFSCME knew that.

As his friend Bill Clinton had said: "He has the heart of a lion."

Acknowledgments

Like the work of a union, the task of writing a book is as much a communal act as the effort of one individual. Over the course of writing this biography, I have been grateful for the help, insight and inspiration that many people have given me.

Of course, I am especially grateful to Jerry and Barbara McEntee for inviting me into this project and for sharing their personal memories of many years of service to AFSCME. I feel honored to have had this opportunity to write such an important part of U.S. labor history with their help and encouragement.

AFSCME Secretary-Treasurer Lee Saunders provided important background on the history of the union throughout his more than 30 years in the struggle for workers rights, along with helpful insight into the contemporary labor movement. Paul Booth, Elissa McBride, Larry Scanlon and Chuck Loveless granted me extensive interviews that helped me better understand the role President McEntee played in shaping the union and the nation's politics over the past generation.

Many AFSCME staff members were crucial to this project. I particularly want to thank Jessica Weinstein, Chris Policano, Blaine Rummel and Belinda Saverino for all their help.

I extend a special note of thanks to Gregory J. King, who set up all of the many interviews I did as part of the research for the book and offered many helpful suggestions and additions to the manuscript as it was produced. I also thank Roger Williams for his careful editing.

Special thanks as well to Carol L. Burnett for her work in keeping us all on schedule and getting the manuscript published. Thanks also to José Noda and Jonathan Kerr for their help in designing the cover and layout of the book, and to Felica Ross-Thompson, who coordinated the photographs selected for this volume.

I also appreciate the help of Johanna Russ, archivist of AFSCME's collection at the Walter Reuther Library for Labor Studies at Wayne State University in Detroit, who provided vital information on the union's history.

I thank Edward J. Keller, past AFSCME Council 13 Executive Director and fellow Philadelphian, for sharing memories of his early days organizing with Jerry McEntee.

I am indebted to many friends who encouraged my work in writing this book, especially Thomas Devaney, Lisa Jarvinen and Wendell W. Young III.

Of course, a special word of appreciation to my entire family, and especially my dear daughter, Siobhan.